EASY AND LUCID GU

TO A KNOWLEDGE OF

RACHEL ABBIE HOLLOWAY LLOYD,

CONTAINING

A CHRONOLOGICAL OUTLINE OF HER LIFE
WITH
EXTENSIVE REFERENCE NOTES TAKEN FROM ORIGINAL SOURCES;

*An historical exploration of recorded and inferred events
in the life of a remarkable chemist:*

TO WHICH ARE ADDED

Suggestions for Future Research and Clarifications of Prior False Inferences,

AND

BRIEF FAMILY HISTORIES

for
Rachel & Her Husband Franklin C. Lloyd

ESPECIALLY DESIGNED FOR PRIVATE LEARNERS AND SCHOOLS

———

BY MARK A. GRIEP.

———

You don't know where you're going until you know where you've been.

———

Lincoln, Nebraska

KEEPER'S COTTAGE PRESS
2014.

Keeper's Cottage Press

ISBN-13: 978-0692290828

ISBN-10: 0692290826

Foreword

My last three years in the presidential succession for the American Chemical Society (ACS) have been an amazing journey. I have done my best to connect with and help support chemistry communities everywhere. As part of my travels, I was privileged to visit the Chemistry Department at the University of Nebraska-Lincoln (UNL). There, during a tour of the Chemistry Department by Dr. Jim Takacs, department chair at that time, I was quite impressed to learn about Rachel Lloyd, the first woman from the U.S. to earn a Ph.D. in chemistry who also became the first female chemistry professor at a coeducational research university in the U.S.A.

Having long been a supporter for women in science, I realized that the University of Nebraska's Chemistry Department Chair in 1887 must have been quite a visionary to hire Dr. Rachel Lloyd. In the 1880's, U.S. graduate schools in chemistry did not even admit women as graduate students, much less offer them faculty positions. Thus, Rachel Lloyd had to leave the U.S.A. to work on her Ph.D. at the University of Zurich despite having successfully completed chemistry courses at Harvard College. This is not too surprising since there were chemistry professors whom I knew who would not accept women for graduate study in the 1970's, almost a century later.

Fortunately, Rachel Lloyd met and worked with a progressive colleague by the name of Hudson Nicholson while both of them were taking summer chemistry courses at Harvard. Professor Nicholson eventually became the Chemistry Department Chair at the University of Nebraska and later offered Dr. Rachel Lloyd a faculty position there.

Upon my return from visiting UNL, I suggested to several people at ACS, including Keith Lindblom, manager of the NHCL program, that Rachel Lloyd and the UNL Chemistry Department be nominated for a National Historic Chemical Landmark (NHCL). I felt it was important to raise awareness about her early achievements as a pioneer woman chemist.

Imagine how absolutely delighted I was to learn that Rachel Lloyd will receive well-deserved recognition at the University of Nebraska's first NHCL ceremony on October 1, 2014. I very much look forward to participating in the symposium on "Women in Science" organized by Dr. Mark Griep, chair of the ACS Nebraska local section and author of this book, as part of the NHCL program to celebrate Dr. Rachel Lloyd's achievements.

It is fitting that this pioneering woman chemist, Rachel Lloyd, receives recognition for her work with many students and for her research that helped lead to the creation of Nebraska's sugar beet industry back in the late 1880's. Her story is part of the history of chemistry and shows the important role that women have played in science. Dr. Lloyd believed that "whatever was worth doing at all was worth doing well," and I have always wholeheartedly shared that same belief.

I am honored to write this Foreword, and I hope you enjoy reading this story of Rachel Lloyd's life as much as I have. Thanks to Mark Griep for conducting the research to write this biography. It should help raise awareness about this inspiring pioneer woman chemist who helped blaze trails for women in science!

Marinda Li Wu, Ph.D.
2013 President
American Chemical Society
August 2014

Preface

In 1997, I learned from my colleague Larry Parkhurst that Dr. Rachel Lloyd had been the first female faculty member in my Chemistry Department at the University of Nebraska-Lincoln. The surprising part of the story was that she joined the Department of Chemistry in the late 1800's (I soon found out it was 1887) at a time when there were very few women scientists. Apparently, there had been an article about her in the Lincoln newspaper in the 1980's that told the story about her research on sugar beets.

Since I am interested in family and local history, I began to dig into her story. A visit to the University of Nebraska Archives unearthed the October 24, 1982 newspaper report about Ann and Stanley Tarbell's article in the *Journal of Chemical Education*. The journalist, Glenda Peterson, began her article by chronicling the prominent historians and government projects that had overlooked Dr. Lloyd's contributions. Notably, Lloyd does not have an entry in *Nebraska Women Through the Years, 1867-1967*, a book prepared for the Governor's Commission on the Status of Women for Nebraska's Centennial in 1967. Since then, I have intermittently scanned old newspapers for her name, read books about the sugar beet industry and early women scientists, visited many archives and history centers (I acknowledge a great debt to the many archivists who helped me), and entered permutations of her name (Rachel Lloyd, Rachael Lloyd, Mrs. Franklin Lloyd, Lloyd Rachel, R. Lloyd, etc.) into innumerable search engines.

In 2012, Dr. Marindu Wu, President-Elect of the American Chemical Society, visited our Department and learned about my department's pride in having Rachel Lloyd as one of our founding faculty. Dr. Wu urged me to submit a nomination for "Dr. Rachel Lloyd and the Nebraska Beet Sugar Industry" as a National Historic Chemical Landmark (NHCL). I did and it was accepted. It will be Nebraska's first NHCL. In October 2014, we will celebrate Dr. Lloyd's life and career with a banquet and a conference. The conference theme of "Women in Science" was chosen because Dr. Lloyd was listed as one of the participants in a conference of that exact same title at the 1893 Columbian World's Fair in Chicago.

This chronological outline of her life was prepared to identify as much primary material as possible for the accompanying NHCL brochure but also to fill in the gaps of her life that had been overlooked by prior researchers. For instance, the title of this book is based on the grammar textbook her father had written before she was born but which had not yet been connected to her life story. I hope you enjoy learning about the life of this remarkable chemist.

Mark A. Griep
Lincoln, Nebraska
September 2014

Table of Contents

Foreword...i

Preface iii

Rachel Abbie Holloway's Early Life, Family, and Career 1

    Map Showing Where Rachel Lloyd Lived in the United States. 1

    Frank and Rachel Lloyd's Philadelphia addresses, 1855-1880................................ 2

    Powers & Weightman's Second Chemical Manufacturing Plant, 1860s................... 3

    Framed print of "Joseph Priestley L.L.D. F.R.S. &c." 1863.................................. 6

    Rachel Lloyd's Headstone, Laurel Hill Cemetery, Philadelphia. 7

    City of Paris, 1866 8

    Mary L. Bonney Rambaut 8

    Charles F. Mabery.. 9

    Rachel Lloyd's signed textbook, 1875 9

    Viktor Merz 14

    Old Chemistry Laboratory, University of Zürich... 14

    Normal School of Science, South Kensington, September 1887 Ad...................... 15

    University of Nebraska's Chemical Laboratory, 1887 16

    Plaster Medallions of Gmelin and Scheele 17

    Grand Island Sugar Beet Factory, 1891 20

    Oxnard Brothers, Beet Sugar Capitalists... 20

    Map showing that sugar beets will grow everywhere in Nebraska, 1891............... 21

    Saccharometer and storage case, probably 1892.. 22

    Professor H. H. Nicholson, 1892... 23

    Qualitative Laboratory, 1892 23

    Sugar from Beets Cartoon, 1892.. 25

    Faculty Photos of H. H. Nicholson and Rachel Lloyd, 1895............................... 27

    Charter for the Nebraska Local Section, March 1895 28

    1894 and 1895 Brochures, Hillside Home School.. 29

    Chemistry Class, Hillside Home School, 1898... 30

    Images of Rachel Lloyd from 1901 and 1895 33

    Rachel Lloyd Frontispiece from Clement Lloyd's 1901 Biography...................... 35

The Robert Smith Holloway & Abigail Taber Family 36

    Cover page from Robert S. Holloway's Grammar Textbook, 1833....................... 36

The Isaac Lloyd III and Hannah Scull Bolton Family... 38

The Clement Lloyd and Irene Gibbens Family 42

    Clement E. Lloyd, Jr., 1890... 42

    Clement E. Lloyd, Jr., 1894... 42

News Articles, Book Extracts, Brochures, & Letters.. 46

About the Author 97

Rachel Abbie Holloway's Early Life, Family, and Career

Rachel Holloway's Early Life

Rachel Abbie Holloway was born January 26, 1839, most likely in Smyrna, Ohio. Most biographies give her birthplace as Flushing but without supporting evidence. The evidence for Smyrna is that her father was postmaster there before Rachel's birth and that her mother died there after Rachel's birth. Rachel was the second child of four by Robert Smith Holloway and Abigail Taber and their only child to survive past age 2. Her parents were teachers. In 1833, Robert privately published a book in St. Clairsville, Ohio, titled *Easy and Lucid Guide to a Knowledge of English Grammar.* It is in the Library of Congress and about a dozen other libraries. When the Mount Pleasant Boarding School was founded in 1837, Robert and Abbie were among the first four teachers. Unfortunately, Robert's poor health caused him to resign at the end of the first year. Afterward, he ran the U.S. Post Office in Smyrna.

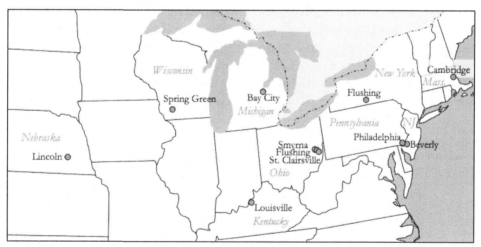

Map Showing Where Rachel Lloyd Lived in the United States.

At this map's resolution, Smyrna, Flushing, and St. Clairsville actually overlay one another.

1844 November 24: Rachel's mother Abby Holloway dies in Smyrna. Abby is buried next to her three children (and later her husband) in the Guernsey Quaker Cemetery, one mile south of Smyrna next to where a Friends Church had been located. Smyrna is located in Harrison County but the Cemetery is located in Guernsey County.

1849 May: Rachel's father marries Deborah Smart

1850 Census: Rachel A., age 11, is living with her father, stepmother, and a relative

1851 June 22: Rachel's father dies. He is buried in Guernsey Quaker Cemetery, near his first wife. He did not leave a will and there is no probate in either Harrison or Guernsey County.

Rachel's stepmother moves to Flushing, where Rachel is enrolled in the Flushing Friends School. Her teacher was Isaac Hall, who later said Rachel was the brightest student he ever taught.

1853: Rachel, age 14, from Flushing enters Westtown School in West Chester, just outside of Philadelphia. It is one the best Boarding Schools run by the Society of Friends. Clement Lloyd was also going to this school and says he knew her but never guessed she would marry his brother Franklin. She may have attended for only one or two years because it was typical to matriculate at age 15 or 16.

Rachel Lloyd's Primary and Secondary Education

Academic Year	Her Age	Institution
youth	until 12	probably home-schooled
1851-1853	13 & 14	Friends School, Flushing, Ohio
1853-1855?	15 & 16	Westtown School, West Chester, Pennsylvania
1855-1856?	17	Friends School, Phil., Margaret Robinson, principal

The years she attended the Flushing Friends School are fairly certain, as is the first year she attended Westtown School. It is not known when she attended Robinson's Friends School.

1854: Rachel's stepmother Deborah Smart Holloway remarries in Flushing, Ohio, to Jehu (or Jehn) Fawcett. She is his third wife.

1855-1859: Rachel is a pupil and then teacher at Miss Margaret Robinson's School for Young Ladies, located on Franklin Street above Race Street in Philadelphia. The School is located on the west side of Franklin Square, about one block from St. Philip's Church. It is during this time that she met Franklin Lloyd who was then employed at Powers & Weightman and it is possible they met at St. Philip's. Margaret Robinson was born in 1820 in New York and graduated from the Albany Female Academy in 1842, one year after it was founded. When its Alumni Association was created a few years later, Robinson served as its first president. Immediately after graduating, Robinson moved to Philadelphia, where she took charge of the Friends School on Franklin Square. She was still teaching there in 1883, 41 years later and was living in a home she owned. One of the most prominent students of the school was Emily Howland, who left in 1857 to join the suffrage movement and to become a teacher at Myrtilla Miner's school for African-American girls in Washington, D.C.

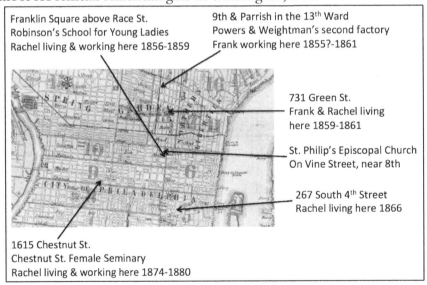

Franklin Square above Race St.
Robinson's School for Young Ladies
Rachel living & working here 1856-1859

9th & Parrish in the 13th Ward
Powers & Weightman's second factory
Frank working here 1855?-1861

731 Green St.
Frank & Rachel living
here 1859-1861

St. Philip's Episcopal Church
On Vine Street, near 8th

267 South 4th Street
Rachel living here 1866

1615 Chestnut St.
Chestnut St. Female Seminary
Rachel living & working here 1874-1880

Frank and Rachel Lloyd's Philadelphia addresses, 1855-1880

As shown on an 1860 map.

<u>Franklin C. Lloyd's Early Life</u>

Franklin C. Lloyd was born January 12, 1832 in Philadelphia. Frank was the third child of nine by Isaac Lloyd III and Hannah Scull Bolton. Isaac was a merchant. Two of their children died as infants, one died at age 9, and another at age 20. The other five married and had children.

1844: Frank enters Central High School, Philadelphia, at age 12

1849 approximately: The family moves to Camden, New Jersey

1850 Census: Franklin age 19 is living in Camden with his parents, siblings, and a servant

1851 April: Frank's mother dies in Camden

1855: His father remarries and they have two children. His father's second wife dies in 1858.

1855 May 13: An adult named "Franklin Lloyd" is baptized in St. Philip's Episcopal Church, located on Vine Street below 8th Street in the Spring Garden section of Philadelphia. Our Franklin would have been 23 years old. The church was formed in 1841 and operated until 1936. This is the same church in which Franklin Lloyd marries Rachel Holloway four years later.

At some unknown date (but 1855 seems likely), Frank began working at the Powers & Weightman pharmaceuticals plant located at Ninth and Parrish Streets in Philadelphia.

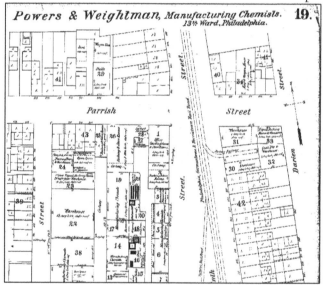

Powers & Weightman's Second Chemical Manufacturing Plant, 1860s.

Located in the 13th Ward at 9th and Parrish Streets. The map is part of the Hexamer General Survey, now in the collection of the Free Library of Philadelphia.

Powers & Weightman of Philadelphia was the first large chemical manufacturing firm in the United States ("Memoir of Thomas H. Powers, read before a meeting of the Philadelphia College of Pharmacy, December 30th, 1878"; "American Chemical Industry" Volume 1 of 6, by William Haynes, 1957, Van Nostrand). It began with two pharmacists, John Farr and Abraham Kunzi, who created it because of the chemical shortage brought on by the War of 1812. Their first compound was sulfuric acid. By 1823, a local malaria epidemic motivated them to produce commercial quantities of quinine, the antimalarial drug. They isolated it from cinchona bark using the method published by Pelletier and Caventou in 1820 (*Ann. chim. phys.* *15*, 287, 337). The company was known for high quality by the time Kunzi retired in 1838 and the company became John Farr & Company. To help him run the business, Farr relied on his chief clerk Thomas Powers and his nephew William Weightman. Thomas Powers was born in Philadelphia, graduated from the Philadelphia College of Pharmacy in 1834, and joined Farr & Kunzi in 1834. Weightman was born in England, and came to Philadelphia in 1829 at age 16 upon his uncle's request. In 1841, the company became Farr, Powers & Weightman. Powers ran the business while Weightman ran the manufacturing plants. The two of them greatly expanded the volume of materials produced until they were running the largest chemical plant in the United States. When Farr died in 1847, the company became Powers & Weightman.

By 1857, Powers & Weightman was producing the following bulk chemicals at their Falls of Schuykill River plant: oil of vitriol (H_2SO_4), nitric acid (HNO_3), muriatic acid (HCl), Epsom salt ($MgSO_4$), blue vitriol ($CuSO_4$), copperas ($FeSO_4$), and alcohol. Most of their profits came from the medicines produced at their second plant at Ninth & Parrish Streets: quinine sulfate, mercurials, morphine salts, and others.

1858 and 1859 McElroy's Philadelphia City Dir.: no entry for either Franklin Lloyd or Rachel Holloway, either indicating they were living elsewhere or with others.

Franklin and Rachel Lloyd's Life Together

Franklin Lloyd and Rachel Holloway marry on May 11, 1859 at St. Philip's Church, Philadelphia.

Reverend Charles DeKay Cooper performs the ceremony. "Mr. Cooper was well known for his vigor and fervor in preaching, and for the many converts he had gained for the Church" according to his 1902 *New York Times* obituary. Cooper was born 1818 in Albany to a physician, earned a degree in engineering from Union College in Schenectady, helped survey railroad routes, saw the light, was ordained in Trinity Episcopal Church in Geneva, and then served at several churches before settling on St. Philip's, where he served from 1847 to 1868. In 1868, he founded Church of the Holy Apostles in Philadelphia, a church that is still active. He retired in 1894.

Even though both Frank and Rachel had been raised in the Religious Society of Friends (or Quakers), they married in an Episcopal church. [*The original church records do not exist. There is only an index to the baptisms (Family History Center, Films 1723744 & 1723745).*]

1860 Census, Philadelphia 13th Ward: Frank Lloyd 28 Clerk, Rachel 21, and servant Anne Miller 21. Anne's race is stated as "Black". She was born in Pennsylvania. Frank's "Value of Estate" is $6000, an amount equivalent to $163,000 in 2014.

1860 McElroy's Philadelphia City Dir.: Lloyd Franklin, clerk, 731 Green Street.

1860: Frank's father's family moves from Camden, NJ, back to Philadelphia, where they live at 824 Lombard Street

1860 October 27: Daughter Fanny L. Lloyd is born. She is named for her aunt who had just died at age 9 in July 1860. Frank and Rachel have been married one and a half years. *Fanny is not listed in the St. Philip's Baptism Index.* Either she was not baptized as an infant, or she was baptized in another church. It was common to wait until children were over seven years old before baptizing them.

1860 November 15 (or 11): According to her death certificate, daughter Fannie dies of "disease of the brain" at age 19 days when they are living at 731 Green Street. This cause of death could mean anything from encephalitis to a brain clot. Fannie is initially buried in Woodlands Cemetery with her aunts, uncles, and cousins. Lot 994 includes her aunt Elizabeth Orrick's family (Newton L., Samuel D., Elizabeth S., _ and Caroline Ross) and her uncle William C.

Lloyd's family (William C., Elizabeth Hopper, Wm C. Jr., Lucy, Helen, and Emily A.).

1861 McElroy's Philadelphia City Dir.: Lloyd Franklin, clerk, N W 9th & Parrish, h 731 Green. Note that Powers & Weightman's pharmaceutical factory is located at 838 N. 9th, and is also described as being on the block bounded by 9th, Parrish, Brown, and Darien Streets.

1861 March: Franklin Lloyd is among the 121 graduates of the Philadelphia College of Pharmacy (*Am. J. Pharm. 33*, p. 95-96). His preceptor was Powers & Weightman, which means he learned the practical aspects of pharmacy on the job. Most men became druggists after spending years helping to run the corner drug shop but Frank's training was undoubtedly more focused on the production side. Also keep in mind that Thomas Powers graduated from this same college in 1834. It is confusing that Frank is not listed among the graduates in "The First Century of the Philadelphia College of Pharmacy, 1821-1921" (1922). There is no evidence Frank was a medical doctor even though he is described in documents from 1893 and 1900 as "Dr. Franklin Lloyd".

In 1893, Rachel Lloyd was interviewed by a reporter for the *Chicago Daily Tribune* who published a feature length article. Here's how the journalist described Rachel's married life: "The girl-wife dearly loved to perch herself, with some bit of sewing, in the deep window of her husband's laboratory, which was a part of their home, and, as she became familiar with the apparatus and watched the experiments with wondering eyes, she little dreamed that the same work would one day be hers in even more extended fields. Widowed when young and with abundant means at her command she chose to travel abroad, where her associations were of the most delightful nature."

1861 April: The Civil War breaks out at Fort Sumter, South Carolina. During the Civil War, the demand for quinine sulfate skyrockets and Powers & Weightman is the primary manufacturer. They didn't raise their price. Instead, the demand created a black market for it when the supplies ran low. As the war ran on, Powers & Weightman introduced a less expensive substitute called cinchonidine sulfate.

1862: Franklin went into business making bricks and retailing coal in Nicetown. In April 1862, he advertised for a "good stone mason" in the newspaper.

Did Frank and Rachel purchase an engraving of Joseph Priestley on one of their early trips abroad? One of the oldest artifacts in the Chemistry Department at the University of Nebraska-Lincoln is a framed engraving of Priestley that was first published in 1863. It is shear speculation to suggest the Lloyds purchased it. However, such a purchase would demonstrate the depth of Frank's affection for a rational unification of science, religion, and politics. After Frank's early death, Rachel may have kept the engraving for similar reasons. Scientifically, Priestley was known for the clever method he used to isolate and characterize eight new gases that he published in the 1770s. He demonstrated the corpuscular nature of matter that allowed John Dalton to devise his atomic theory in the early 1800s that became widely known and accepted in 1855. Politically, Priestley wrote that science should be used to improve the quality of life and that governments should act to maximize the civil liberty and happiness of the majority of its members. After he voiced support for the rationalism behind the French Revolution in 1791, English royalist rioters burned down his home in Birmingham and he decided to immigrate to the United States. From 1794 until his death in 1804, he lived in Northumberland, Pennsylvania, where he established the first Unitarian Church in America and wrote many books and pamphlets about this new religion.

Framed print of "Joseph Priestley L.L.D. F.R.S. &c." 1863

This print is in the University of Nebraska-Lincoln Chemistry Department. L.L.D. means Doctor of Laws and F.R.S. means Fellow of the Royal Society. Conrad Cook was the engraver. William Mackenzie of Glasgow printed it in 1863.

1863 and 1864 McElroy's Philadelphia City Dir.: no entry for Franklin or Rachel Lloyd

1863: Frank and Rachel moved to Bangor Township, Michigan, located adjacent to Bay City, where he supervised a sawmill, salt works, and barrel factory. They built a house but lived in it for less than two years. According to his obituary, it was this work in "unbroken country, which afforded the largest field for his industry and talent." According to the Hannum family history, "Franklin was engaged in the lumber business, Bay City." He also taught Sabbath School and preached. "The tearful tribute of that community, after two years' acquaintance…has in it an eloquence of testimony which heroes might envy."

1865 Census and Statistics of the State of Michigan: Franklin Lloyd in Bangor is running a steam evaporation salt works on 175 acres. In 1864, he invested $20,000 (equivalent to $190,000 in 2014) and produced 1,800 barrels of salt. The lumber mills throughout the area generated plenty of wood chips to provide fuel to create steam. It is not known whether the $20,000 investment was entirely his own.

1865 May-June: The Civil War ends.

1865 August 20: Son William C. Lloyd is born in Philadelphia. He is named for his uncle and his cousin. Rachel must have traveled home to Philadelphia without Franklin. It is not known where she stayed. *William is not listed in the St. Philip's Baptism Index.*

1865 October 7: According to his death certificate, Willie dies in Philadelphia of "jaundice" at age 1 month and 20 days. This cause of death refers to the symptom of yellow skin. It was most likely due to a hepatitis infection since there was an epidemic of infantile hepatitis deaths in the 1860s across the United States. The visitation took place at 505 Arch Street, location of the undertaker William H. Moore. Willie is buried at Woodlands Cemetery near his sister Fannie.

1865 October 6 (or 7): Franklin dies in Bangor (or Bay City), Michigan, age 33. His body must have been transported to Philadelphia where there was a visitation for him on October 13 at William H. Moore's at 505 Arch Street. Franklin is buried on October 13th alongside his two children, Fanny and Willie, in Woodlands Cemetery.

There is an obituary for Franklin published in a Philadelphia newspaper that is written by R*, who

Clement Lloyd wrote "was one of his [*Frank's*] life-long friends." R* writes, "As a son and brother, always thoughtful and affectionate, as a friend, of well tried and never failing constancy. And as a husband, the tenderness with which his first vows were breathed seemed to be only deepened and ripened by the lapse of time."

Young Widow of Means but of Poor Health, Philadelphia and Europe (1865-1873)

1865: The records for Franklin Lloyd's probate no longer exist because the Bay County records were consumed by fire in 1870. It is possible that his salt business in Michigan was worth more than the $20,000 investment due to the post-war Reconstruction boom. Since the investment may not have been his alone, it is safe to assume Rachel inherited at least $6000.

1866 November 13: "Mrs. Frank Lloyd" purchases lot 76 in section 9 of Laurel Hill Cemetery while living at 267 South 4th Street. Laurel Hill is one of the earliest park cemeteries and was the first cemetery to receive status as a National Historic Landmark. It was founded in 1836 along the banks of the Schuykill River in Philadelphia.

1867 March 13: The remains of Franklin, Fanny, and Willie are removed from Woodlands Cemetery to Laurel Hill Cemetery. The headstone is a hip tomb in the Gothic style. In 1900, Rachel was buried with her husband and two children.

Rachel Lloyd's Headstone, Laurel Hill Cemetery, Philadelphia.

This Gothic style hip tomb has the name RACHEL carved on the long face and FANNY in the trefoil. On the other side, FRANK is carved on the long face and WILLIE is in the trefoil. Photos by Mark Griep.

1867-1872: According to Rachel's obituaries, she spent several years abroad after she was widowed. The evidence suggests she traveled back and forth several times. During her first trip, she sought relief from rheumatism (inflammation of the joints) and neuralgia (intermittent pain along a nerve, and often in the face). Later in life, she gave a talk about her personal reminiscences of the Dutch painter Lawrence Alma-Tadema. Since he settled in London in 1870, it is reasonable to suppose she met him during this time period.

In 1868, she is back in Philadelphia living on Fourth Street near Spruce Street. It was during this time that she became active in St. Peter's Protestant Episcopal Church by teaching Sunday school. (The yard surrounding this church is filled with headstones and was featured in the movie *National Treasure*, 2004, starring Nicolas Cage.) She also visited the children in their homes to look after their physical health. Reverend Thomas Davies became rector at St. Peter's in 1868 and wrote that "she knew each child by name, maintained perfect order without the slightest show of authority, and imparted instruction so as to win all their hearts."

1872 April 27: Mrs. Rachel Lloyd sailed from New York to Liverpool on the *City of Paris* steam ship. Her health had begun to fail again so she was heading to Germany for water treatment.

City of Paris, **1866**

1873: Rachel returned home when the economic crisis of September 1873 left her penniless. The panic was set off by the bankruptcy of Jay Cooke & Co., which had over-invested in railroad construction after the Civil War. By 1875, over 18,000 businesses had failed. By 1876, the unemployment rate was 14%.

<u>Chemistry Teacher at the Chestnut Street Female Seminary, Philadelphia (1873-1880)</u>
<u>Chemistry Student at the Summer Course in Chemistry, Harvard College (1875-1883)</u>

1873-1880: Rachel Lloyd is the chemistry teacher at the Chestnut Street Female Seminary, the most progressive school for girls in the country. Rachel told her brother-in-law Clement Lloyd that her motive to "take up the study of chemistry as her life work was because her husband having been a fine chemist, she felt that she could not honor his memory better than to follow in his footsteps, believing, as she told the writer, she had his approval." Miss Mary L. Bonney and Miss Harriet A. Dillaye founded the school in 1850. The school's inaugural catalog indicates that, "the course of study will include all branches constituting a thorough scientific and literary education." It was at 525 Chestnut Street, but became 1615 Chestnut Street when the city renumbered.

Mary L. Bonney Rambaut
circa 1898 from *Emma Willard and Her Pupils: Or, Fifty Years of Troy Female Seminary, 1822-1872*, by Mary J. Mason Fairbank, 1898

Many years after she retired, Mary Lucinda Bonney married Mr. Rambaut and she then played a pivotal role in obtaining rights for Native Americans. Eventually, three documents from her Chestnut Street school made their way into the archives of the American Baptist Historical Society under the heading: "Rambaut, Mary Lucinda Bonney 1816-1900 RG-1237 Educator". The first is a "Ledger of the Female Seminary, 1878-1888" but a researcher reported that it contains entries related to business and not employees. The second is an autobiographical sketch of Mrs. Rambaut, written in 1886. The third item is a history of the Chestnut St. Seminary dictated by Mrs. Rambaut in 1894. This third item is partially reproduced in the final section of this book for its insights about the founding and operation of the school.

1875 Summer: Harvard University Catalogue, p. 162:
    Course in Chemistry: Lloyd, Mrs. Franklin, *Teacher, Philadelphia, Pa.*
Charles F. Mabery, a chemistry graduate student at Harvard, taught the Harvard summer course in chemistry. In 1883, Mabery joined the faculty at Case Institute, now Case Western Reserve, in Cincinnati. Two of his students later founded Dow Chemical. Mabery retired in 1911.

	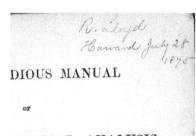
Charles F. Mabery	**Rachel Lloyd's signed textbook, 1875**
This photo was taken in 1912, long after he taught the Summer Course. Reproduced by permission of Case Western Reserves Archives.	*Lloyd used this book in her first Harvard Summer Course. It is in the UNL Chemistry Department. Photo by Mark Griep.*

1875 July 28: On this date, "R. Lloyd" signed her copy of "Qualitative Chemical Analysis" by Charles W. Eliot and Frank H. Storer, Third Revised Edition, New York: Van Nostrand, 1874. She used this book in her Harvard Summer Chemistry Course.
1876 Summer, Harvard University Catalogue, p. 154:
    General Chemistry: Lloyd, Mrs. Franklin, *Teacher, Philadelphia, Pa.*

Rachel Lloyd's Attendance in the Harvard Summer Courses

1875	Course in Chemistry
1876	General Chemistry
1877	Quantitative Analysis
1878	no listing for Lloyd
1879	Advanced Quantitative, Including Organic Analysis, and Special Experimental Methods; she also attended the Botany Course
1880	Advanced Quantitative Analysis and Organic Chemistry (led to her 1881 paper)
1881	Advanced Quantitative Analysis and Organic Chemistry (led to her 1882 paper)
1882	no listing for Lloyd
1883	Advanced Quantitative Analysis and Organic Chemistry (led to her 1884 paper)

1877: The Association for the Advancement of Women (AAW) published its first list of members. The five members living at "1615 Chestnut" were Frances E. Bennett, Mary L. Bonney, Henrietta Dillage [*Dillaye*], Helen R. Foote, and Mrs. Franklin Lloyd. They probably joined when the AAW held its fourth annual meeting in Philadelphia in October 1876. Maria Mitchell co-founded the organization in 1873, was its president in 1875, and chaired its Science Committee until she died in 1889. Mitchell was a prominent astronomer who was the first woman to join the American Association for the Advancement of Science in 1850. The AAW was the first of many organizations that Rachel Lloyd joined or founded. In 1890 and 1891, she was a member of the AAW Science Committee.

Rachel Lloyd's Memberships and the Year Admitted

Association for the Advancement of Women	1876?
Deutsche Chemische Gesellschaft zu Berlin	1886
Chemical Society of London [*or English Chemical Society*]	1887?
Haydon [*originally Hayden*] Art Gallery, Lincoln	1888 (founding member?)
American Association for the Advancement of Science	1889 Fellow
[*Robert*] Browning Club, Lincoln	1890 (founding member)
Scientific Club, University of Nebraska	1890 (founding member)
American Chemical Society, New York	1891 (second woman)
Nebraska Academy of Sciences, Lincoln	1891 (founding member)
University Camera Club, University of Nebraska	1892 (founding member)
National American Woman Suffrage Association	1893
American Chemical Society Nebraska Section, Lincoln	1895 (founding member)

1877 Summer, Harvard University Catalogue, p. 188:

> Quantitative Analysis: Lloyd, Mrs. Franklin, *Teacher, Philadelphia, Penn.*

1878 Summer, Harvard University Catalogue, p. 200:

> General Chemistry: Palmer, Kate, *Teacher of Biology in Girls' High School* (she also took Botany); Lloyd is not listed. In 1884, Kate Palmer and Rachel Lloyd taught at the Louisville School of Pharmacy for Women.

1879 Summer, Harvard University Catalogue, p. 216:

> Advanced Quantitative, Including Organic Analysis, and Special Experimental Methods: Lloyd, Mrs. Franklin, *Teacher,* Philadelphia, Pa. (she also took Botany).

1880 Gospill's Philadelphia City Directory: Chestnut St. Seminary, 1615 Chestnut, *Mary A. Bonney & Harriet A. Dillaye, Principals*; Lloyd Rachel, *teacher, h 1615 Chestnut*

1880 Federal Census in Philadelphia: Rachel Lloyd, 40, school teacher, is living at the Chestnut Street Female Seminary with the Principal, Matron, three other teachers, a bookkeeper, and seven servants. It is not clear where the girls are boarding. The staff was a bit larger than in the 1870 Census when it was Bonney, Dillaye, and four teachers. Helen Foote was Dillaye's niece and one of her longest-term employees. Helen was a teacher in 1860 and 1870 but a bookkeeper in 1880. Frances Bennett was perhaps the second long-term teacher since she appears in the 1870 and 1880. The housekeeper and six domestics are living next door. In 1870, Miss Bonney's real estate value is $45,000. The 1860 group was about the same size as the one in 1870. It consisted of Bonney, Dillaye, four teachers, a housekeeper, seven servants, and 25 girls "in school" between the ages of 10 and 17. The 1860 girls were from the following states: Pennsylvania 13, New York 4, Indiana 2, and one each from Illinois, Louisiana, Maryland, Missouri, Vermont, and Virginia.

The 1880 Federal Census of the Chestnut Street Seminary

Name,	Relation, Marital Status, Sex, Race, Age, Birthplace,	Occup.,	Father's Birthplace, Mother's
Mary Bonney,	Self, S, F, W, 63, NY,	Principal Of School,	MA, MA
Henrietta Dillaye,	Other, S, F, W, 63, NY,	School Teacher,	France, NY
Elizabeth Kilburn,	Other, W, F, W, 41, VT,	Matron,	VT, VT
Rachel Lloyd,	Other, W, F, W, 40, OH,	School Teacher,	VA, MA
Frances Bennett,	Other, S, F, W, 37, NY,	School Teacher,	CT, NY
Lydie Remy,	Other, S, F, W, 23, —Belgium,		School Teacher,

Hellen Foote,	Other, S, F, W, 47, NY,	Book Keeper,	CT, NY
Eloise Carr,	Other, S, F, W, 19, PA,	Servant,	Ireland, Ireland
Kattie Coan,	Other, S, F, W, 35, Ireland,	Servant,	Ireland, Ireland
Mary Dunn,	Other, S, F, W, 34, NY,	Servant,	Ireland, Ireland
Hannah McGheean,	Other, S, F, W, 45, Ireland,	Servant,	Ireland, Ireland
Ellen McNamee,	Other, S, F, W, 21, Ireland,	Servant,	Ireland, Ireland
Martha Willett,	Other, W, F, B, 46, NJ,	Servant,	MD, NJ
Mary Collins,	Other, S, F, W, 26, PA,	Servant,	Ireland, Ireland

Marital Status is either Single or Widowed, one servant is African American, and the average servant's age is 32.

1880 Summer, Harvard University Catalogue, p. 221:
> Advanced Quantitative Analysis and Organic Chemistry: Lloyd, Mrs. Franklin, *Teacher*, Clifton Springs, N.Y. (this is the first summer she met Hudson Nicholson)
> Quantitative Analysis: Nicholson, H. H., A.M. *(Lawrence Univ.), Teacher*, Peru, Neb.

1880 August: C. F. Mabery attends the Boston meeting of the American Association for the Advancement of Science, subsection of chemistry. On Saturday, August 28, he "described some substituted acrylic acids recently investigated by himself with the co-operation of Mrs. R. Lloyd." This also happens to be the meeting at which an infamous dinner was held on August 27 during which the "ribald proceedings were taken down by a male stenographer, privately printed, and distributed to members as *The Misogynist Dinner of the American Chemical Society.*"

1883: The Chestnut Street Female Seminary becomes the Ogontz School when they move into "Ogontz," Jay Cooke's former mansion. In 1888, Miss Bonney and Miss Dillaye retire. In the 1950s, the Ogontz School becomes co-educational. In 2003, it becomes Penn State Abington.

Lady Principal of Foster School for Girls, Clifton Springs, New York (1880-1882)

1880: Rachel Lloyd becomes the Lady Principal at the Foster School for girls in Clifton Springs, NY

1881: Charles F. Mabery and Rachel Lloyd publish their first paper together, "XI.—On the diiodbromacrylic and chlorbromacrylic acids" in *American Chemical Journal* (volume 3, pages 124-129). The first footnote says "Communicated by the Authors. This research was conducted in connection the Summer Course of Instruction in Chemistry at Harvard College.—C.F.M." It was the first paper in this prominent journal to be authored by a woman.

1882 February 8: Charles F. Mabery and Rachel Lloyd publish their second paper together, "XVIII.—Dibromiodacrylic and chloriodacrylic acids" in *American Chemical Journal* (volume 4, pages 92-100). The first footnote says "The investigations described in the following papers were made under my supervision, and they formed a part of the work in the Summer Course of Instruction in Chemistry for 1881.—C. F. MABERY."

1882 July: Mrs. Rachel Lloyd is no longer lady principal at the Foster School. Miss Ada L. Howard resigned her position as president of Wellesley College to replace her.

Instructor of Chemistry and Physics at Hampton College for Women, Louisville (1882-1885?)
Instructor of Chemistry at Louisville School of Pharmacy for Women (1884-1885)

1882 Summer: Harvard University Catalogue does not list Lloyd as taking the summer course

1882 November: Mrs. Rachel Lloyd advertises that she is recently Lady Principal of the Foster School in New York and is now instructor of Chemistry and Physics at Hampton College in Louisville, Kentucky. She has formed classes for experimental work in General Chemistry,

Qualitative and Quantitative Analysis. Miss L. D. Hampton founded the Hampton College for Women in 1882. It was located at 316 West Walnut Street in Louisville, Kentucky, and operated at least until 1896. Another instructor was Mrs. Laura Belle Cross who earned her A.B. at Hampton in 1883 and then taught there. Mrs. Cross attended the Harvard Courses in Botany during the summers of 1883 and 1886.

1883 Caron's Louisville City Directory: Lloyd, Rachel, teacher Hampton College. She may have lived at the College. There is no entry for Louisville School of Pharmacy for Women.

1883 Summer: Rachel Lloyd from Hampton College attends her last Summer Course in Chemistry at Harvard. In total, she attended seven of the past eight summers. Hudson Nicholson from the University of Nebraska also attended this summer course. It was the second time the two of them attended together, the first being 1880 when Hudson was chemistry professor at Nebraska's Peru Normal School.

1883 October: Louisville School of Pharmacy for Women opens its doors with Mrs. Rachel Lloyd as Professor of Chemistry and Secretary of Faculty. The other woman faculty member was Miss Kate Palmer, Professor of Botany. J. P. Barnum, M.D., Professor of Pharmaceutical and Analytical Chemistry founded the School. Dr. Barnum argued that women were suited for Pharmacy work but that the requirements of training on the job prevented them from becoming druggists. At first, the School was located at 34 Schurmann Block. By 1887, it was in the Polytechnic Building. It operated nine years until the 1891-1892 academic year at which time 52 students were registered. The School closed due to insufficient patronage. The following pharmacy schools had women on the faculty in the late 1800s ("A Historical Perspective on Women Pharmacy Faculty," *American Journal of Pharmaceutical Education 63*, pp. 402-405, 1999). (1) Louisville School of Pharmacy for Women had Rachel Lloyd as a chemistry teacher and Kate Palmer as a botany teacher; (2) Ferris Institute had Anna G. Pease from 1886-94; (3) Purdue had Katherine Golden from 1894-98; and (4) The University of Michigan had Louisa Reed Stowell in the early 1880s. The first woman faculty member with a degree in pharmacy was Josephine R. Barbat. She graduated from the California College in Pharmacy in 1884 and served as an assistant in botany around 1889.

1884: Charles F. Mabery and Rachel Lloyd publish their third and final paper together, "XLI.— On α- and β-chlordibromacrylic acids" in *American Chemical Journal* (volume 6, pages 157-165). The first footnote says "The results described in papers XLI, XLII, and XLIII were obtained under my direction in the summer course of instruction in chemistry for 1883.—C.F.M." The next paper is by Charles F. Mabery and H. H. Nicholson "XLII.—On β-dibromdichlor-propionic and β-dibromacrylic acids" in *American Chemical Journal* (volume 6, pages 165-170).

1884 Spring Semester: The first session at the Louisville School of Pharmacy for Women is taught to 13 women and two men. Of these, Miss Fauntine Vetter of Louisville, Miss Delia W. Marble of Owensboro, and Mr. R. T. Creason were the first three graduates of the school in August 1884. I can find no further material on Vetter. Miss Marble was probably the daughter of the other male student, Mr. Dwight H. Marble. Delia's interest was clearly botanical because she became an active member of the New York Botanical Garden where she catalogued the plants of the West Indies in 1904. By 1933, Delia was Curator of Geology at Barnard College. A fourth student in the very first semester was Mrs. W. L. Buzan, who received a full diploma in July 1888, and who became an active druggist in Louisville. She may have been related to C. A. Buzan, who was an unlicensed but practicing druggist in Louisville. Mrs. Buzan suffered the effects of an explosion in December 1899 while she was preparing amyl nitrate in her shop. She died in 1905. A fifth student in that first semester was Fayette Barnum, who was probably the daughter of the School's Dean Dr. J. P. Barnum. Fay became a prominent Louisville artist.

1884 Caron's Louisville City Directory: Louisville School of Pharmacy for Women, J. P. Barnum, dean, 34 Schurmann Block; there is no entry for Rachel Lloyd.

In 1884, Bryn Mawr College in Pennsylvania began accepting women professors on its faculty. Rachel Lloyd applied to fill a chemistry position and had the most laudatory testimonial from Dr. Mabery but was denied the position because she lacked a degree. She decided to get one in the most direct way possible for a woman, which is to enroll at the University of Zurich. It was the only university that offered graduate research training in the sciences to women.

Graduate Student of Chemistry at the University of Zurich (1885-1887)

1885 May: Rachel Lloyd obtains a passport from the U.S. State Department. She lives in Kentucky and her witness is Mary Floyd Welman. The physical description says she is 45 years, five foot tall, has a broad and high forehead, blue eyes, small and straight nose, small mouth, short chin, brown hair, fair complexion, and full face. According to her great grandson John Hultgren, Miss Welman graduated from Hampton College (probably in 1883) and then began teaching there. She was 24 years old in 1885 and married in 1888.

Among her personal papers, Clement Lloyd found her description of the ship's journey. The ship was named the *Trave* and the destination was Bremen, from which she took a train. After they left the dock, she wrote "A look around on the vast expanse, and the ship which at the pier seems so huge, so unyielding, becomes an atom in comparison, is tossed like a feather upon old ocean's bosom, and one realizes how little is between him and eternity."

1886 December: Rachel writes a letter to her brother-in-law Clement in which she describes the holiday festivities in Zurich. She signs the letter "Chellie."

1887 February: Rachel Lloyd earns her Ph. D. in chemistry from University of Zurich, working with Dr. Viktor Merz. Merz was born in Odessa, Ukraine, in 1839. He moved to Zurich in 1852, where he attended Industrieschule and then studied chemistry first at the Technical University and then the University of Zurich. He earned his doctorate in 1862 from Zurich while doing research at Munich with Justus Liebig during the 1861-62 academic year. He earned his habilitation in 1866 and was appointed professor of chemistry in 1870. Merz retired in 1893, moved to Basel and then Lausanne, where he died in 1904. He authored about 170 publications and was remembered as an outstanding teacher, dedicated to science, endowed with a perfect memory, and linguistically gifted. He knew German, French, English, Russian, and Italian.

Viktor Merz

Photo from "Prof. Dr. Viktor Merz" (1904) Verhandlungen der Schweizerischen Naturforschenden Gesellschaft, p. 60

THE OLD CHEMISTRY LABORATORY OF THE UNIVERSITY OF ZÜRICH

Old Chemistry Laboratory, University of Zürich

Photo from a brochure.

1887 December: Rachel Lloyd's thesis work "Ueber die Unwandlung höherer Homologen des Benzolphenols in primäre under secondäre Amine" is published in *Berichte des deutschen chemischen Gesselschaft* (vol. 20, pp. 1254-1265). In 1888, her translation was published in *University Studies* (vol. 1, no. 2, pp. 1-22), a journal to promote research at the University of Nebraska.

1887 March: The U. S. Congress establishes Experiment Stations by passing the "Hatch Bill". The result is that land grant colleges are to establish agricultural experiment stations "to promote scientific investigation and experiment respecting the principles and applications of agricultural science." Said stations shall publish bulletins or reports at least once in three months. The sum of $15,000 is appropriated to each state to pay the expenses of conducting experiments and the printing and distribution of the bulletins.

Unknown Position in the Normal School of Science, London (1887)

1887 February? to April?: Dr. Lloyd worked briefly as an assistant for Dr. Frankland at the Normal School of Science and Royal School of Mines in the South Kensington area of London. The schools were located in the building that is now the Victoria and Albert Museum. She was living at 32 Dorset Square, which was a 2-mile walk northeast through Hyde Park. In 1881, the Schools came under the direction of Thomas Henry Huxley, the prominent academic biologist and strong proponent of Charles Darwin's Theory of Evolution. Huxley would have been the person who hired Lloyd. The School's name was continually in flux but its purpose was always to provide systematic training for schoolteachers. In 1887, they offered four semesters each of lectures and laboratory in chemistry, physics, biology, and mechanics. They also offered courses in geology, metallurgy, mining, agriculture, and astronomy. In 1907, the Schools moved to a new building and joined the Imperial College of London system.

Normal School of Science, South Kensington, September 1887 Ad.

This advertisement is from Chemical News, published in London.

Professor of Chemistry at the University of Nebraska (1887-1894)

1887-1888: First year at University of Nebraska

1887 April 15: At a faculty meeting, the faculty request that the Board of Regents offer Rachel Lloyd the position of Acting Associate Professor of Analytic Chemistry at a salary of $1500 per annum for one year starting July 1, 1887. It is approved. Henry Hudson Nicholson, Chair of Chemistry and Physics, sends her a telegram offer.

1887 April 16: Rachel Lloyd sends her letter of acceptance from 32 Dorset Square, London. It arrived in Lincoln on April 26.

1887 April 25: Rachel Lloyd accepts the offer in a telegram to Nicholson.

1887 July: Lloyd arrives in Lincoln to become Associate Professor of Chemistry at the University of Nebraska. Her salary was $1500 plus $500 as the assistant chemist at the Agricultural Experiment Station. Professor Rosa Bouton later wrote that Dr. Lloyd, "had a deep rich voice with good carrying qualities. She spoke distinctly and her choice of words was excellent." Bouton also wrote: "She loved her work and succeeded in getting her students to do the same. Her personality was very strong, and at the same time very attractive. One recognized her at once as a woman of broad culture and refinement. Dr. Lloyd had the power of making personal friends of her students and of awakening in them an enthusiasm akin to her own for the study she so much enjoyed. Her influence over young people was wonderful. Accordingly, her greatest work was that of a teacher. Many are the alumni and former students of this University who stand ready to hear loving tribute to her memory."

1887 August: An article in the *Woman's Tribune* by Ada L. Bittenbender congratulates the University of Nebraska for hiring Dr. Rachel Lloyd. The article describes Lloyd's research at Harvard, teaching at Hampton College, and her Ph.D. at University of Zurich. Bittenbender moved to Nebraska with her lawyer husband in 1879. In 1883, they began jointly practicing law in Lincoln. Bittenbender was active in the Lincoln chapter of the Women's Christian Temperance Union and served as its President for several years. In the 1890s, Bittenbender founded the Nebraska Women Suffrage Association and spent many years lobbying the Nebraska State Legislature on this issue.

15

Nicholson's Office

Nicholson's Lab

Lloyd's Office

Lloyd's Lab

University of Nebraska's Chemical Laboratory, 1887

Photo from Science volume 10, p. 82.

1887 August: Nicholson description of the Chemical Laboratory building is published in *Science* magazine (volume 10, pages 82-84). Nicholson was the Chair and sole instructor until Dr. Lloyd's arrival. Dr. Lloyd's office and lab were located on the second floor while Nicholson's were on the third. The building was ready in late summer 1886.

The plans and construction of the Chemical Laboratory were tracked over two years by the student newspaper *The Hesperian.* There was a great deal of interest because it was the second campus building. To come up with ideas for the design, Nicholson visited laboratories at the University of Michigan, the University of Ohio, and the Case School of Applied Science (where Charles Mabery was located) during the summer of 1884. In the summer of 1885, Nicholson traveled to Europe to purchase apparatus, some of it made to order. In February 1886, 169 books arrived for the chemistry library, located just south of Nicholson's office. There were 39 volumes of *Chemical News*, 56 volumes of *Chemisches Central-Blatt*, 28 volumes of *Berichte der deutschen chemischen gesellschaft*, 23 volumes of *Fresenius Zeitschrift fuer analytische Chemie*, 9 volumes of *Jahresbuch der reinen Chemie*, 6 volumes of Kopp's *Geschicte der Chemie*, and one French-German-English Dictionary. In June 1886, the chemical library received an addition of about 150 volumes, most of them in German.

Medallions of Gmelin and Scheele adorned the front face of the Chemical Laboratory. They were located on either side of the south entrance in the band separating the second and third floors. Even though the building is gone, these two medallions survive. I have not been able to discover why the building's designer, H. H. Nicholson, choose to memorialize these two chemists. They are interesting choices because they encapsulate a great deal of chemistry. Leopold Gmelin was a Chemistry Professor at the University of Heidelberg who studied the chemistry of digestion. In 1817, he published the first edition of his three-volume *Handbuch der Chemie* and it quickly became the major chemistry textbook. By the fourth edition, it had grown to nine volumes and Gmelin had adopted the atomic theory. He also devoted much more space to the growing discipline of organic chemistry and introduced the terms *ester* and *ketone.* Karl Wilhelm Scheele was a Swedish apothecary who discovered barium, chlorine, manganese, molybdenum, nitrogen, oxygen, and tungsten, but is not credited with discovering of any of them.

Plaster Medallions of Gmelin and Scheele

The medallions were located on either side of the Chemical Laboratory entrance in the band between the second and third floors. The medallions are still in the Department. Photos by Mark Griep.

In 1919, the Chemistry Department moved to Avery Hall and the Chemical Laboratory became Pharmacy Hall. When Pharmacy Hall was torn down in 1959 to make way for the Sheldon Museum, the Gmelin and Scheele medallions were recovered and given to the Chemistry Department, which displayed them in the chemistry library. When the Chemistry Department moved to Hamilton Hall in 1970, the medallions were stored in its basement, where they were forgotten until 2001 when the storage room was renovated. While showing them to my colleagues, one of them told me there were also busts on stands in the library of Jacobus van't Hoff (discoverer of tetrahedral carbon) and Jöns Jakob Berzelius (developer of the chemical notation we still use today—element symbols followed by a number representing its ratio within the compound). I have not been able to locate any photos of the chemistry library during the Avery Hall days.

1888 June 13: "Mrs. Lloyd, according to the chancellor, is an infidel," reported the *Omaha Daily Bee* on their front page. Chancellor Manatt said it the night before in a secret meeting with four regents. The chancellor had asked Regent Chairman Charles Gere to ask the faculty whether to reappoint Mrs. Lloyd. Gere said he did ask the faculty. Manatt insisted he had not. The next day, the *Bee* interviewed Chancellor Manatt. He denied he said Mrs. Lloyd was an infidel. When the *Bee* corroborated with two regents that he did, it predicted the end result would be firing of the chancellor. They were right. On June 15, the Chancellor hoped he could end the debacle by explaining to the Regents that Mrs. Lloyd "is spoken of as an excellent Christian lady." The alumni association petitioned for his removal and within months he was gone.

1888: Rachel Lloyd is promoted to Professor of Analytic Chemistry. Rachel's friend and colleague, Professor Charles Bessey, becomes Acting Chancellor.

1888-1889: Second year at University of Nebraska

1888 October: Rachel Lloyd's translation of her own graduate thesis is published in *University Studies* (vol. 1, no. 2, pp. 1-22), a journal from the University of Nebraska initiated by Chancellor Manatt. Her paper is published after he was fired from the University.

1888: Dr. Lloyd joins the Hayden Art Club _____during its first year and remains an active member until 1893. This Club was the precursor for the Sheldon Museum of Art.

1888 November: Prof. Nicholson forms a reading club in current chemical literature. According to *The Hesperian*: "The members of the club are all greatly interested in the work, and the weekly discussions are very profitable. The movement is to be commended."

1888 November: Dr. Lloyd lectures on "Ceramics" for the Hayden Art Club.

1889 Lincoln City Dir.: Lloyd Mrs. Rachel, associate Prof. at Chem Lab, N 13th 445

1889 January: Prof. Rachel Lloyd gives a presentation to the Nebraska Board of Agriculture about the first year's analysis of the sugar content in beets grown by two Grand Island farmers. The result was very favorable and she calls for more experimentation. Nicholson and Bouton both wrote that the audience of farmers was completely enthralled throughout. In a letter to Clement Lloyd, Hudson Nicholson wrote, "Mrs. Lloyd followed me. Now I suppose that some of those men labored under the impression that a woman and a wash tub ought to be inseparable. At any rate they seemed surprised that a woman could calmly walk up on the platform and read a scientific paper. You should have seen the thrill of life that ran through the assembly…At the close of the paper they applauded to the echo—none of the rest of us received that, and before the day was over, Mrs. Lloyd had been requested to read her address in another city."

1889 March 1 based on the *Minutes of the Society of the Hall in the Grove, Lincoln*: The Chautauqua Literary and Scientific Circle of Lincoln took a field trip to the Chemical Laboratory at the invitation of Dr. Rachel Lloyd. The visit began with a violin and coronet duet by graduate student Elton Fulmer (B.Sc. 1887; M.A. 1890) and undergraduate Jacob Frankforter. Then, Prof. Lloyd introduced Prof. Nicholson who lectured and performed demonstrations on water. The Lincoln branch of the Chautauqua Society was founded in September 1888 and chaired by Miss Phoebe Elliott, a prominent schoolteacher and very active member of the board of education. Elliott Elementary School is named in her honor. Other founding members of the Lincoln Chautauqua were Mrs. D. L. Anderson, Mrs. Mina F. Metcalf, Mrs. A. L. Metcalf, and Mrs. Ellen R. Rollins.

Spring 1889: Mrs. Rachel Lloyd is elected to the Hayden Art Club's Board of Directors and serves for one and a half years.

1889 March: H. H. Nicholson sends a letter to hundreds of Nebraska farmers asking them to grow sugar beets and then to record the following: Kind and variety of seed planted; number of acres planted; date of planting; kind of soil; method of cultivation; time of harvesting; cost per acre; and kind of season.

1889 March: The Nebraska Legislature offers a bounty on sugar from plants grown in the state.

1889 April: Two varieties of sugar beets, Lane's Imperial and Vilmorin, arrive at the University from the Department of Agriculture. Nicholson and chemistry undergraduate Herbert Marsland (B.Sc. 1890) distribute them to farmers across the state.

1889 Summer: Nicholson and Marsland collect cultivation data from the farmers, who are directed to send their beets to the University by November 1 for analysis.

1889-1890: Third year at University of Nebraska

1889 August: Sugar beets begin arriving at the University for analysis. By December, there are beets from thirty counties.

1889 October: Mrs. Rachel Lloyd is elected a Fellow of the American Association for the Advancement of Science. AAAS was founded __ in 1848 by 87 practicing scientists. The organization's goal is to promote scientific dialogue as the means to foster greater scientific collaboration, more efficient use of resources, and an increase in scientific progress. Martha Mitchell, a prominent astronomer, was admitted in 1850 as the first female member. AAAS suspended operation during the Civil War. When they resumed operation, they opened membership to anyone but simultaneously created the category of Fellow to recognize members who were prominent scientists. It is a great honor to be elected an AAAS Fellow. AAAS began publishing *Science* in 1880, a weekly journal that features science news and peer-reviewed articles. Today, *Science* is among the most prestigious general science journals.

1889 November: The community leaders of Grand Island propose locating a beet sugar factory here because the 1888 season had been such a success. Before it can be laid before the Grand Island citizens for a vote, $60,000 is raised.

1890 Lincoln City Dir.: Lloyd Mrs. Rachel, associate professor of chemistry, n 13th 445

1890 January 11: Prof. Rachel Lloyd attends a Browning memorial meeting at the home of Mr. and Mrs. A. J. Sawyer in Lincoln. Robert Browning died in December 1898 and was a renowned Victorian poet. Andrew Sawyer was Lincoln mayor from 1887 to 1889 who wrote an important history of Lincoln in 1912. At the meeting, the group decides to organize a Browning Club. The attendees included H. H. Nicholson who was elected treasurer, Dr. A. Marine was president, Mrs. C. H. Gere and Mrs. R. H. Oakley were vice presidents, and English professor Lucius A. Sherman was corresponding secretary. Others in attendance were geology professor Lewis E. Hicks and Mrs. DeWitt L. Brace. The Browning Club of Lincoln operated until at least 1907.

1890 March: Mrs. Lloyd attends another meeting of the Browning Club where she is assigned to the committee to complete its constitution.

1890 April: H. H. Nicholson, A. M., and Rachel Lloyd, Ph. D. publish "Sugar Beet Series I. Experiments in the Culture of the Sugar Beet in Nebraska" in *Bulletin No. 13* of the Nebraska Experiment Station on April 1. It is 81 pages long and was their first publication on this topic. It describes the results from the 1889 season and begins with the sugar content in beets grown at the University Experiment Station by Mr. J. G. Smith, Assistant Agriculturist. The percent sucrose was very low at 11.4, 2.25, 2.25, 5.14, 9.22, and 5.63 but it didn't seem to discourage anyone from wanting to grow more beets. The report ends with an acknowledgment, "In the chemical work of this bulletin we have been greatly aided by Mr. T. H. Marsland, who made a large number of beet analyses. To Mr. Elton Fulmer [*B.Sc. 1887; M.A. 1890*], Miss Rosa Bouton [*B.Sc. 1888; M.A. 1893*], and Mr. H. B. Duncanson [*B.Sc. 1892; M.A. 1894*], we are under obligation for valuable assistance."

1890: The Grand Island Beet Sugar Factory is built and ready for operation in 1890. The Oxnard Brothers, who were located in California, managed it. It was the Nation's third such factory. It operated until the 1960s by which time it was the longest operating beet sugar factory in the United States. The first beet sugar factory in the United States was built in Alvarado, California, in 1879. It operated until at least the 1930s. The second beet sugar factory was built in Watsonville, California, in 1888 but it shut down in 1898.

Grand Island Sugar Beet Factory, 1891

Oxnard Brothers, Beet Sugar Capitalists

Both photos are from the Stuhr Museum Library, Grand Island.

Record of the Beet Sugar Industry in Nebraska, 1890-1895

	Tons of beets worked			Granulated sugar produced (lbs.)			No. of growers		
Year	G.I.	Norfolk	Total	G.I.	Norfolk	Total	G.I.	Norfolk	Total
1890	4,414	--	--	736,400	--	--	607	--	--
1891	10,868	8,179	19,047	1,415,800	1,318,700	2,734,500	408	204	612
1892	13,055	10,725	23,780	2,110,100	1,693,400	3,803,500	249	490	730
1893	11,150	22,625	33,775	1,835,909	4,107,300	5,943,200	135	181	310
1894*	drought	25,633	25,633	--	5,556,100	5,556,100	--	534	534
1895	24,343	31,194	55,537	2,983,400	5,395,500	8,378,900	619	698	1317

*In 1894, the tonnage at Grand Island was so small due to the drought that the beets belonging to the Grand Island plant were worked up at the Norfolk factory. This information is from *The American Sugar Industry* by Herbert Myrick, 1899, New York: Orange Judd Company.

1890-1891: Fourth year at University of Nebraska

1890: Dr. Lloyd is elected to the Hayden Art Club Board of Directors for a second year. She resigns in November for an unknown reason.

1890 October: Prof. Rachel Lloyd is elected to the Science Committee of the Association for the Advancement of Women. The other AAW members from Lincoln are Mrs. Eleanor Brace, wife of the University of Nebraska Physics Professor, Mrs. Lura Leavitt, wife of the Grand Island Sugar Beet Factory Manager, Miss Sarah Wood Moore, Professor of Art at the University of Nebraska, Mrs. Sarah Weeks, and Mrs. Mary Wing. In the meeting notes, Dr. Rachel Lloyd "reports a valuable paper on the manufacture and testing of sugar-beet sugar" (Wolcott, H. L. T., 1891, "Committee on Science" in *Report of the Association for the Advancement of Women's 18th Congress in Toronto, Canada, in October 1890*).

1891 Lincoln City Dir.: Lloyd Rachel, tchr. State University, b[oards] 606 n 16th; her previous house at 445 N. 13th was probably acquired and demolished as the University expanded its footprint.

1891: The second beet sugar factory in Nebraska is erected in Norfolk in 1891. It is built and managed by the Oxnard Brothers. Unfortunately, the temperature, rainfall, humidity, and soil conditions are not well suited to sugar beets. In 1905, the plant shuts down and the equipment is moved to the plant in Lamar, Colorado.

1891 April: H. H. Nicholson, A. M., and Rachel Lloyd, Ph. D. publish "Sugar Beet Series II. Experiments in the Culture of the Sugar Beet ___in Nebraska" in *Bulletin No. 16* of the

Nebraska Experiment Station on April 15. It is 98 pages long and was their second publication on this topic. It describes the results of sugar beet experiments during the 1890 season. The report ends with an acknowledgment, "In closing, we wish to acknowledge our obligations to the Burlington, Union Pacific, and the Elkhorn railroad companies, for their courteous co-operation which enabled us to reach parts of the state otherwise inaccessible to us; to the Oxnard Bros., for their kindness in adding to our stock of seed for free distribution; to the farmers of the state, and also to the field agents, Messrs. H. B. Duncanson [*B.Sc. 1892; M.A. 1894*], H. A. Senter [*B.Sc. 1893; Univ Heidelberg Ph.D. 1896*], and Edward E. Nicholson [*B.Sc. 1894; M.A. 1896*], for their zeal and fidelity in carrying out their instructions even at the sacrifice of personal comfort."

1891 Summer: According to September issue of *The Hesperian*, "The professors of chemistry were at work in their laboratories during the greater part of summer." According to the October issue, "Professor Lloyd took a short vacation about the middle of the summer and made a trip to the eastern states" while "Professor Nicholson took the last two weeks of the summer months…to attend…the national science convention and the meeting of the national chemistry society." Rosa Bouton had just earned her M.A. in Chemistry at Nebraska and she accompanied him. While in Boston for the ACS meeting, she visited the lab of Mrs. Ellen Swallow Richards of MIT, who was creating the field of sanitary chemistry.

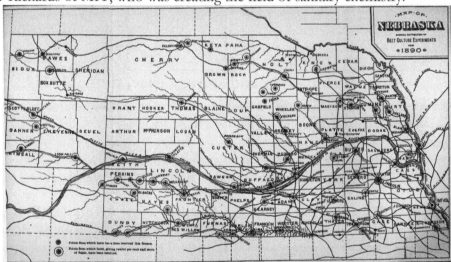

Map showing that sugar beets will grow everywhere in Nebraska, 1891

From Sugar Beet Series II Bulletin based on the results from 1890 growing season.

1891-1892: Fifth year at University of Nebraska

1891 October: For the second year, Prof. Rachel Lloyd is a member of the AAW Science Committee. In the meeting notes, Mrs. R. Lloyd "has been elected professor at Lincoln, Neb., after a course of study in Europe. Until some radical change is made on this line, women are virtually excluded from this pleasant and honorable avenue" (Mitchell, M., 1892, "Committee on Science" in *Report of the Association for the Advancement of Women's 19th Congress in Grand Rapids, Michigan, in October 1891*).

1891 December: At the Hayden Art Club, "Mrs. Dr. Rachel Lloyd gave a personal reminiscence of artist Alma-Tedenia [*sic*] that was very entertaining." Dutch painter Lawrence Alma-Tadema settled in London in 1870. Lloyd must have ___met him while she was in Europe between

1870 and 1872.

1892 Lincoln City Dir.: Lloyd Rachel, tchr. State University, r. 1504 S

1892 February 15 to September 15: Dr. Lloyd is Acting Chair of Chemistry, Director of the Chemical Laboratory, and Director of the Experiment Station while Nicholson embarks on a seven-month "trip to Europe in the interests of the Beet Sugar Industry of this state." The University paid $600 to cover his entire trip. On February 27, Nicholson attended the joint meeting of the beet sugar societies of Hannover and Braunschweig. He then toured the sugar beet schools of Germany and ended his trip by observing the sugar beet fields of France during harvest.

1892 March 18: Lloyd submits the Department's annual request for funds to the Chancellor "in the absence of the efficient and energetic director of the department."

1892 April 4: Lloyd submits another request for funds to the Chancellor. It seems that Nicholson worked out a deal for purchasing special equipment that wouldn't involve middlemen during his visit to the School for Sugar Industry in Braunschweig.

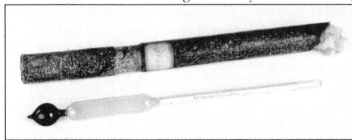 

Saccharometer and storage case, probably 1892

It is possible that the UNL Chemistry Department's collection of 8 saccharometers were among the items purchased through the Braunschweig School for Sugar Industry. The paper labels in them says "M K & M", which means Max Kaehler & Martini of Berlin, a glassblowing company active from the mid-1870s until the 1920s. The earliest publication to mention saccharometers made by this company is from 1892 (M. Schöpff, Berichte der deutschen chemischen Gesellschaft 25, 3642-3647). Photos by Joel Sartore.

1892 April: H. H. Nicholson and Rachel Lloyd publish "Sugar Beet Series III. Experiments in the Culture of the Sugar Beet in Nebraska" in *Bulletin No. 21* of the Nebraska Experiment Station on March 1. It is 44 pages long and was their third publication on this topic. It describes the results of sugar beet experiments during the 1891 season. The report ends with an acknowledgment, "In closing, we wish to acknowledge our obligations to the Burlington, Union Pacific, and the Elkhorn railroad companies, for their courteous co-operation which enabled us to reach parts of the state otherwise inaccessible to us; to the Oxnard Bros., for their kindness in adding to our stock of seed for free distribution; to the farmers of the state, and also to the field agents, Messrs. H. B. Duncanson, H. A. Senter, and Edward E. Nicholson, for their zeal and fidelity in carrying out their instructions even at the sacrifice of personal comfort."

1892 *Sombrero*, the University of Nebraska Yearbook:
    On page 12, Photo of Prof. H. H. Nicholson, Director of the Agricultural Experiment Station.

Professor H. H. Nicholson, 1892

Archives and Special Collections, University of Nebraska-Lincoln Libraries.

On page 15: HUDSON H. NICHOLSON, M. A., *Professor of Chemistry*, Director of the
    Experiment Station, Harvard and Heidelberg, Germany. Author of B-
    Dibromchlorpropionic and B-Bromdichloracrylicacids. Investigations in the Culture of
    Sugar Beet in Nebraska.

On page 15: RACHEL LLOYD, Ph. D., *Professor of Analytic Chemistry*, Ph.D., Zurich, 1887;
    Harvard College; South Kensington Schools of Science and Royal School of Mines,
    London, 1887; Author of "Certain Acrylic Acids;" "The Conversion of Some of the
    Homologues of Benzol-Phenol into Amines;" Investigations in the Culture of the Sugar
    Beet in Nebraska.

On page 15: Photo of the Qualitative Laboratory

Qualitative Laboratory, 1892

*This room was on the second floor. The photographer is facing north while positioned in a doorway in the
center of the building. Dr. Lloyd's office was located through the door ahead and then to the right. Her lab
was located immediately to the right of the photographer. Archives & Special Collections, UNL Libraries.*

On page 19: H. ELTON FULMER, M. A., *Instructor in Chemistry*, B. Sc., 1887; M. A. U. of N., 1889. Φ. Δ. Θ.

On page 22: JANITORS, ETC.

    RICHARD ADAMS, Chemical Laboratory

On page 35: GRADUATE STUDENTS.

    Rosa Bouton, Chemistry, Sabetha, Kan. [*B.Sc. 1888; M.A. 1893*];

    Clarence C. Fletcher, Chemistry, Lincoln [*B.Sc. 1891; M.A. is unrecorded*]

    Abel E. Wagner, Sugar Beet Chemistry, Beatrice [*B.Sc. 1891; M.A. is unrecorded*]

On page 165: SCIENTIFIC CLUB. Organized October 1890.

    OFFICERS. [*from chemistry*]:

    Secretary-Treasurer, Rosa Bouton.

    MEMBERS [*from chemistry*]:

    Sam Avery [*Samuel B.Sc. 1892; M.A. 1894; Univ. Heidelberg Ph.D. 1896*].

    J. B. Beecher [*Jesse Bradford; B.Sc. 1893; M.A. 1896*].

    Rosa Bouton [*Rosa; B.Sc. 1888; M.A. 1893*].

    R. S. Bulla [*Rolland Stanton; M.A. 1893*].

    Mary Fossler [*Mary Louise; B.Sc. 1894; M.A. 1898*].

    Elton Fulmer [*H. Elton; B.Sc. 1887; M.A. 1889 but his thesis is missing*].

    Mariel Gere [*Mariel Chapman; M.A. 1899*].

    P. L. Hibbard [*Paul L.; B.Sc. 1892*].

    R. S. Hiltner [*Robert Silver; B.Sc. 1894; M.A. 1893*].

    Dr. Rachel Lloyd.

    Prof. H. H. Nicholson.

    E. E. Nicholson [*Edward Everett; B.Sc. 1894; M.A. 1896*].

    H. A. Senter [*Herbert Almon; B.Sc. 1893; Univ. Heidelberg Ph.D. 1896*]

On page 181: The "Sugar from Beets" cartoon by "Edna Hyatt, Mch 4, 92." (see image on next page)

1892 June 2: Lloyd submits the Department's annual report to the Chancellor. It includes a summary of the sugar school.

1892: *Science* magazine publishes Professor Lloyd's full-length report about the sugar school at the University of Nebraska. Mr. Lyon taught the sections on sugar chemistry, beet sugar technology, and sugar beet culture. Professor DeWitt Brace taught sections on light, polarization, and the principles of the polariscope and different forms of saccharimeters.

1892 Summer: Nicholson spends the entire summer in Europe. Lloyd spends part of her summer in Iowa. When she is visiting Mr. and Mrs. Weeks in the Black Hills of South Dakota, she suffers partial paralysis on her right side. She never fully recovered.

Sugar from Beets Cartoon, 1892

Prof. Nicholson talks to Prof. Lloyd, who is spilling a dark liquid on her dirty apron. The dark liquid is probably the brick red copper oxide solid produced during Fehling's reaction for free glucose. The disheveled state of Dr. Lloyd's apron does not jibe with Rosa Bouton's March 1900 memorial in which she said: "Dr. Lloyd was neatness personified. In her dress, in the arrangement of her lecture table, in her laboratory, everything was exceptionally neat and orderly." Archives & Special Collections, UNL Libraries.

1. Mabery, C. F., and Lloyd, Mrs. R. (1880) Abstract: "Diiodbromacrylic and Chlorbromacrylic Acids" *American Chemical Journal 2*, 276.
2. Mabery, C. F., and Lloyd, Rachel (1881) "XI.—On the Diiodbromacrylic and Chlorbrom-acrylic Acids" *American Chemical Journal 3*, 124-129.
3. Mabery, Charles F., and Lloyd, Rachel (1882) "XVIII.—Dibromiodacrylic and Chlorbrom-iodacrylic Acids" *American Chemical Journal 4*, 92-100.
4. Mabery, Charles F., and Lloyd, Rachel (1884) "XLI.—On a- and b-Chlordibromacrylic Acids" *American Chemical Journal 6*, 157-165.
5. Lloyd, Rachel (1887) "Ueber die Umwandlung höherer Homologen des Benzolphenols in primäre und secondäre Amine" *Berichte der Deustchen Chemischen Gesellschaft 20*, 1254-1265.
6. Lloyd, Rachel (October 1888) "I.—On the Conversion of Some of the Homologues of Benzol-Phenol into Primary and Secondary Amines." *[Nebraska] University Studies* (1888-1892) *1*, no. 2, pp. 1-22.
7. Lloyd, Prof. Rachel (1889) *Annual Report Nebraska State Board of Agriculture For 1888*, pp. 80-84.
8. Nicholson, H. H., and Lloyd, Rachel (1890) Sugar Beet Series I. "Experiments in the Culture of the Sugar Beet in Nebraska" pp. 1-81, Bulletin 13, April 1, 1890.
9. Nicholson, H. H., and Lloyd, Rachel (1891) Sugar Beet Series II. "Experiments in the Culture of the Sugar Beet in Nebraska" pp. 1-98, Bulletin 16, April 15, 1891.
10. Nicholson, H. H., and Lloyd, Rachel (1892) Sugar Beet Series III. "Experiments in the Culture of the Sugar Beet in Nebraska." pp. 1-44, Bulletin 21, March 1, 1892.

1892-1893: Sixth year at University of Nebraska

1892 Fall: The University Camera Club is formed and Prof. Lloyd is on the Executive Committee.

1892 October: The Nebraska Student Newspaper reports that six university men are now employed at sugar stations of the west: two in Kansas, two in Schuyler, and two in Norfolk.

1893 Lincoln City Dir.: Lloyd Rachel, prof. State University, r. 1504 S

1893 April: "Mrs. Rachel Lloyd" is elected a board member of the Lincoln Savings Bank

1893 April: The *Chicago Daily Tribune* publishes a very long biography of the noted chemist Rachel Lloyd, Ph. D. The article says she was the first American woman to acquire a Ph.D. from a foreign university, the first to introduce experiments in Girls' Schools, and describes how her early life led her to the position she has attained.

1893 May 16: "Dr. Rachel Lloyd, University of Nebraska" is the first listed member of a discussion following a talk titled "Women in Science" by Dr. Mary Putnam Jacobi, a prominent New York physician. The talk and discussion took place in the Hall of Washington at the Columbian World's Fair in Chicago. This fair opened the day before. The other advertised discussants were Dr. Mary A. D. Jones, Louise Reed Stowell, and Mrs. Leander Stone. According to the published notes from this talk, Dr. Julia Holmes Smith, a prominent Chicago physician, read Dr. Jacobi's speech. It consists of very brief summaries of many women who were or are engaged in all manner of scientific endeavors. There were no quotes from either Dr. Lloyd or Louise Reed Stowell during the discussion, suggesting they did not attend.

1893: Rachel Lloyd of Nebraska gave $1 (called an Auxiliary fee) to the National American Woman Suffrage Association, which was in its 25th year. She paid $1 again in 1894. The group's President was Susan B. Anthony and its Honorary President was Elizabeth Cady Stanton. The other Nebraska supporters were Mary H. Williams $98, A. D. Williams $13, Helen M. Goff $10, Ellen D. Harm $6, Mrs. Kate Williams $5, J. D. Evans $5, C. M. Nye

$4.50, Mrs. S. B. Colson $4.50, Mary S. Hayward $2, Sophia C. Hoffman $1, Zinka Kiulalia $1, and E. C. Wentworth $1. Clara Bewick Colby was the sole Nebraska representative to attend the Conferences in February of 1893 and 1894. Colby published *Woman's Tribune*, a suffragist's magazine begun in Beatrice, Nebraska, that eventually relocated to Washington, D.C.

1893-1894: Seventh year at University of Nebraska

1893 September: From *The Hesperian*, "Dr. Lloyd has returned greatly improved in health after a pleasant summer on the Atlantic coast, Nova Scotia and Prince Edward's Island."

1893 October: The *Daily Inter Ocean*, a newspaper published in Chicago, runs a full-feature biography of Dr. Rachel Lloyd. It is an abbreviated version of the article that appeared in the *Chicago Daily Tribune* earlier in the year.

1893 December: From *The Hesperian*, "Prof. Lloyd spent her vacation in Fremont, as guest of Etta and Vesta Gray." Vesta graduated in 1893 although probably not in chemistry, practiced law in Fremont, and became one of its leading citizens.

1893 December: From *The Hesperian*, "Prof. Lloyd has recently organized a class in History of Chemistry."

1893 December: From *The Hesperian*, "Prof. Nicholson left for Florida. The professor has been ill for some time."

1894 Lincoln City Dir.: Lloyd Rachel, tchr. State University, r. 1504 S

1894 May 23: From *The Hesperian*, "Mrs. Rachel Lloyd left Sunday for Chicago where she will make her home in the future." She is not listed in the Chicago City Directories of 1895 or 1896.

1894 June 9 in the *Hesperian*: "Because of ill health, Dr. Lloyd has decided to resign her position as associate professor of Chemistry." "Dr. Lloyd will go to the Atlantic Coast."

1894 June 30: Prof. Lloyd officially resigns from the University of Nebraska.

1895 *Sombrero*, the University of Nebraska Yearbook: On page 17, Photos of Faculty "H. H. Nickelson" and "Rachel Lloyd" by "ER Wright, Phil."

Faculty Photos of H. H. Nicholson and Rachel Lloyd, 1895

Archives and Special Collections, University of Nebraska-Lincoln Libraries.

1895 March: Nicholson leads the Nebraska members of the American Chemical Society in their request to create a Nebraska Local Section. They are granted a charter on March 22, 1895 and become the seventh local section. The first column of names on the charter lists H. H. Nicholson, T. L. Lyon, Rosa Bouton, H. A. __Senter, and R. Lloyd.

The American Chemical Society.

CHARTER FOR A LOCAL SECTION.

THE BOARD OF DIRECTORS OF THE AMERICAN CHEMICAL SOCIETY have considered a written application received *March 22 1895*, for the establishment of a Local Section of said Society at *Lincoln, Nebraska*, to embrace the territory of ; the said application being signed by the following chemists, all members of the Society in good standing, viz :

H. H. Nicholson	Elton Fulmer	R. S. Hiltner
T. L. Lyon	John White	P. L. Hibbard
Rosa Bouton	Edward E. Nicholson	F. F. Tucker
H. A. Senter	Jesse B. Becker	W. H. Baird
R. Lloyd		W. H. Robinson

As it has been satisfactorily shown that the establishment of the said Section will tend to the advancement of chemistry and will be for the interest of the American Chemical Society, THE BOARD OF DIRECTORS, in conformity with Article *Ten* Section of the Constitution, and by the authority therein conferred, hereby authorizes the formation of a Local Section of said Society, in accordance with the terms of said application ; such Local Section to have all the rights and privileges of Local Sections under the Constitution and By-Laws of the Society, and to be subject to all provisions of said Constitution and By-Laws as now existing or as hereafter modified by general vote of the Society.

The said applicants and such members of this Society as they may elect or appoint as their associates or successors, shall be regarded as members of the said Local Section and are hereby authorized to direct and control the affairs of the Section.

Edgar F. Smith *President.*   Charles E. Munroe

Harvey W. Wiley   Edward Hart

Peter E. Cushman   W. McMurtrie

A. A. Breneman   C. F. Chandler   } Board of Directors.

Charles A. Doremus   F. E. Dodge

Chas. F. McKenna

John Howard Appleton   Albert C. Hale, *Secretary.*

NEW YORK. *Feb. 25* 1895.

Charter for the Nebraska Local Section, March 1895

The signatures of the American Chemical Society officers are originals but the names of the local section members were written by one hand. At some point, the charter was glued to a piece of heavy cardboard causing it to darken. The above image was cleaned using Adobe Photoshop. The original is still in the Chemistry Department.

Instructor of Science at Hillside Home School, Spring Green, Wisconsin, 1894-1895

1894 August: From *The Hesperian*, "Mrs. Rachel Lloyd to teach science in all grades at Hillside Home School." "Her health is greatly improved." Jane and Ellen Lloyd-Jones founded the Hillside Home School in 1887. The school was co-educational and children learned by doing. Jane and Ellen were Frank Lloyd Wright's maternal aunts. He designed the building as his first important commission and his two children attended it. The school closed when his aunts retired in 1919. He replaced the building in 1928 with a new one designed for architecture students. It is located near Taliesin outside the__city of Spring Green, west of Madison.

1894 and 1895 Brochures, Hillside Home School

Mrs. Rachel Lloyd is mentioned in both brochures. The covers are reproduced by permission from the Wisconsin Historical Society (WHS call number PH-6676).

1894 *Proceedings of the Nebraska Academy of Sciences*, List of Members: RACHEL LLOYD, Hillside, Wisconsin; Teacher of Chemistry in Hillside Home School.

1894-5 Hillside Home Brochure, page 16: "Important additions have been made in the science department of the school for the coming year. The science room has been fitted up for laboratory work in experimental physics and chemistry, and Mrs. Rachel Lloyd, Ph. D. of the University of Zurich, and late professor of chemistry in the University of Nebraska, has been secured to take charge of the scientific instruction in all grades."

One of the Hillside Home School graduates of 1895 was Florence Fifer (later Bohrer). It seems likely she would have taken Dr. Lloyd's chemistry course in her final year. Florence's father had been Governor of Illinois from 1888 to 1892. In 1955, Florence wrote that her favorite subject at Hillside was mathematics and that she disliked Latin even though Mr. Hugenholtz was an excellent teacher. She also wrote the following about one of her schoolmates, "Because the race question is still with us, this comes to my mind—my Hillside experience with the controversial subject. Among the students was one colored girl, Mabel Wheeler of Chicago [*who also graduated from Hillside in 1895*]. Her father was an attorney, and the members of her family belonged to Uncle Jenk's [*Jenkins Lloyd-Jones*] "All Souls" Church. Mabel lived in the farm home of one of the Uncles, and everything went smoothly until scarlet fever descended on the household [*this must have been Fall 1894*]. The Aunts immediately called the older girls together in the library for a conference. There were no vacant rooms and, unless someone rooming alone in the Home Building would take Mabel in as a roommate for the remainder of the term, she must return to Chicago. Aunt Nell called for a volunteer, my hand went up, and that night Mabel moved in and shared my room, not only for the term but the rest of the school year. She was a very bright girl, talented and popular among the students. She later graduated from the University of Chicago and went on to teach in one of the universities for negroes in the South. [*Florida State College for Women, Tallahassee*]" In 1898, Florence married Jacob Bohrer and they had two children. Florence became involved in many progressive causes and served as the local director of the Red Cross during the Great War. In 1924, she ran for Illinois State Senator and won without the assistance of the Republican Party. She served two terms as the Illinois' first woman Senator, during which time she focused on the laws governing children (From *Wisconsin* ___*Magazine of History* Spring 1955 and *Illinois History* April

1998).

Chemistry Class, Hillside Home School, 1898

These girls are probably using the chemical apparatus ordered for the school by Mrs. Rachel Lloyd in 1894.
The photo is reproduced by permission from the Wisconsin Historical Society (WHS-25556).

1894 October 25 to December 3: Mrs. Lloyd from "Hill-Side" paid eight visits to Dr. Marcus
Bossard, the physician who served this area. On her fourth visit in five days, October 29, she
paid 50¢ for a 2-oz. bottle of something. Dr. Bossard never indicated which medication was
dispensed. Next, Mrs. Lloyd paid 50¢ for 3 oz. of something on November 4, November 24,
and December 3. The final entry from February 1895 indicates she paid her $19.50 bill in full
"by cash." Did Mrs. Lloyd catch the scarlet fever that was in the area in Fall 1894? Scarlet
fever affects primarily ages 2 to 10 but was so epidemic in the nineteenth century that it also
affected older children and even adults. The most common treatment for children was to let
the disease run its course while applying wet towels to their bodies. An adult would be less
likely to take themselves out of commission or to want someone to watch over them. The
most common physician's treatment was bloodletting either through the use of leeches or
cutting. The next most common treatment was a mercurial, a drug containing mercury.

1895 *Proceedings of the Nebraska Academy of Sciences*, List of Members: RACHEL LLOYD, Hillside,
Wisconsin; Teacher of Chemistry in Hillside Home School.

1895-6 Hillside Home Brochure, page 17: The faculty includes RACHEL LLOYD, *Natural Science*.
She probably did not teach at the Hillside Home for a second year.

Retired and living in Philadelphia, 1896-1899

Clement Lloyd wrote that Rachel spent one year at a progressive school in Wisconsin before
returning to Philadelphia, where she lived except for the last nine months of her life.

1896 and 1897 *Proceedings of the Nebraska Academy of Sciences*, List of Members: There is no entry for
Rachel Lloyd.

1897 McElroy's Philadelphia City Dir.: There is no entry for Rachel Lloyd. She was probably living
with someone.

1897 June: Rachel Lloyd's brother-in-law Clement Lloyd speaks at a Westtown School Alumni
Reunion about his time at the school in the 1850's. He was a few years younger than Rachel at
Westtown but he writes that she "is deserving of especial mention, she having made Chemistry

her principal study since, in which she achieved success and distinction, and who, as Prof. Rachel Lloyd, Professor of Chemistry, at Lincoln, was largely instrumental in introducing Sugar Beet Culture into that State." It is likely that Rachel attended this reunion.

1897 June: "Mrs. Rachel Lloyd, a former lady principal" attended a reunion of the Foster School in Clifton Springs. The news report said, "Mrs. Lloyd is well known for her specialties in chemistry and physics, having been one of the first American women to obtain a degree at the University of Zurich, Switzerland." Clement Lloyd later wrote that she "thoroughly enjoyed meeting her former pupils and friends." One of the highlights of the evening was when someone read a poem titled "Old Maids" that named many of the attendees and that "shows what a jolly time they all had." The first verses mention the marriages of the Thompson sisters, Laura Hyde, Kate Weaver, Lillie Hoyt, Emma Cochran, Christmas Norton, and Jennie P. Betts. Then, it mentions Rachel Lloyd.

> But somewhat of sorrow would cloud our delight,
> And much of our bliss be destroyed,
> Were it not for the presence among us to-night
> Of our very dear friend, Mrs. Lloyd.

Final eight months

1899 July: Rachel Lloyd moved to Beverly, New Jersey, to live with an old family friend, Mrs. Anna Scattergood. Anna, age 62, was living with her mother, age 87, at this time. Anna Johnson was born in December 1837 in New York and had married David Scattergood in 1860 in Beverly, New Jersey. David was an engraver who created many images including some based on Edgar Allen Poe's works that are highly sought after. David was nine years older than Anna and died in the mid-1890's. Rachel may have met the Scattergoods years earlier during a visit to Clement Lloyd's house in Beverly.

1899: The third beet sugar factory in Nebraska is erected in Ames (near Fremont) in 1899. It is built and managed by the Standard Beet Company. Its president is Mr. Heyward G. Leavitt, who had been the original manager of the Grand Island plant but who then helped set up the Norfolk plant. Leavitt had convinced the Standard Land and Cattle Company to raise sugar beets on its land in Ames so they could feed the beet waste to the cattle. In 1899, 1900, and 1901, the town of Fremont celebrated the "St. Eeb Ragus" Carnival and Street Fair. Unfortunately, there were several years of excessive rainfall that lowered the beet yield. The plant shut down in 1906 because it was too difficult to convince farmers to grow beets. In 1910, the factory was dismantled and moved to Scottsbluff, where it was enlarged. Within the next 17 years, five more factories were built in the North Platte Valley: Gering in 1916, Bayard in 1917, Mitchell in 1920, Minatare in 1926, and Lyman in 1927.

Rachel Lloyd dies March 7, 1900, in Beverly, New Jersey. Her death certificate indicates the cause is "heart failure; a signal of paralysis." She is interred in the Laurel Hill Cemetery with her family on March 10, 1900. Clement's son R. Louis Lloyd arranges the burial details and for the name of RACHEL to be cut into the face of the tomb.

Memorials

1900 March 14: Acting Chancellor Bessey gives a tribute to Mrs. Rachel Lloyd to students in the University chapel. He provides a few _____interesting details about her early life, describes the day Nicholson called him into his office to ask what he thought of hiring a woman chemist, and says she was an inspiration to students. His most moving lines are: "There still lingers on this campus like a sweet perfume the memory of her devoted life. It is your good fortune to be here where these memories still influence your lives."

1900 March: Rosa Bouton read an address to the Nebraska Local Section that included this insight into her personality: "She believed that whatever was worth doing at all was worth doing well. Whatever she undertook, and she undertook many things, she did it in the best way. I think I never knew any one who took more care of the details than she; consequently every one knew that whenever she did a piece of work it would be well done in every particular. And since she did so much work it necessarily follows that she was an indefatigable worker. Eight o'clock in the morning usually found her at the laboratory, and she seldom left at night before six, many times returning in the evening to continue her labors."

1900 April 22: Hudson Nicholson wrote a letter to Clement Lloyd saying: "The death of Mrs. Lloyd has been to us like the loss of one of our own family. Not only in my immediate family, but through the University circle has her loss been an almost personal loss…We are considering now the project of placing in the chemical laboratory a tablet commemorating her life and work here." There is no evidence the tablet was ever created.

1900 October: Clement Lloyd finishes writing his biography of his sister-in-law Rachel Lloyd and has it privately published. In my search for a copy of this book, I discovered it is not among Clement Lloyd's papers in the Swarthmore College archives even though Clement's son, R. Louis Lloyd, had donated papers to Swarthmore College that "descended in the family" including, "Some notes in handwriting of Clement E. Lloyd." Clement's book is also not in the libraries of Case Western Reserve Archives, Chemical Heritage Foundation, Chicago History Museum Library, ETH-Zurich Archives, FamilySearch.org, New York Public Library, Pennsylvania History Museum Library, State of Ohio Archives, U. S. Library of Congress, University of Kentucky Archives, University of Nebraska Archives, or University of Pennsylvania Library.

1901 January 10: *The Times* of Philadelphia writes a four-paragraph summary of Clement Lloyd's biography of Prof. Rachel Lloyd. The most interesting line is, "The book, which is handsomely printed bearing a beautifully engraved portrait of the late Professor Lloyd on the initial page, contains a complete sketch of her life, and reproduces many of her letters." The newspaper reproduced the engraving, which is obviously based on the 1895 yearbook photo. Her eyes were lightened, her gaze was oriented to the viewer, and her name was removed.

1901 January: *The Westonian*, Westtown Alumni Association's publication, announces that Clement E. Lloyd of Philadelphia "has printed for private distribution, a brief memorial of his sister-in-law, Rachel Lloyd."

1901 January 30: The *New York Daily Tribune* prints a four-paragraph obituary of Dr. Lloyd based on a short sketch of her life that was recently published. They must have been referring to Clement Lloyd's biography. The interesting lines are, "Beet sugar is now a leading industry of Nebraska, and Professor Nicholson says that Dr. Lloyd is entitled to the greater part of the credit as she did most of the work."

Images of Rachel Lloyd from 1901 and 1895

The 1901 engraving in The Times *(left) compared to the 1895 Yearbook photo (right)*

1901 April: C. F. Mabery publishes his obituary of "Professor Rachel Lloyd, Ph.D., Zurich" in the *Proceedings of the American Chemical Society* (vol. 23, pages 84-85), which was celebrating its 25th anniversary. Along with a description of her life and career, he writes: "Dr. Lloyd possessed remarkable energy and force of character, combined with broad culture and great mental ability. To natural refinement and a sympathetic nature she united the culture of the best society and extended foreign travel. These qualifications with a strong and attractive personality, and the power of making personal friends of students, rendered her teaching very effective."

Dr. Lloyd's Place in History

1916 June 22: The University of Nebraska Chemistry Department places a photo of "Prof. Rachel Lloyd, the second head" and other items in a time capsule in the cornerstone of the New Chemical Laboratory building (renamed Avery Hall in 1948).

1969: Robert Manley publishes his two-volume "Centennial History of the University of Nebraska." In volume 1, he writes, "Professor H. H. Nicholson and a brilliant woman professor, Rachel Lloyd, who had joined the faculty in 1888 [*1887*], presided over the Chemical Laboratory."

1970: The Chemistry Department moves into the newly constructed Hamilton Hall and the faculty are encouraged to leave the past behind. Ignoring the charge, Prof. James Carr brings the collection of older analytical instruments, including the saccharometers that Dr. Lloyd must have used.

1982 September: Ann and Stanley Tarbell publish a biography of Dr. Lloyd in the *Journal of Chemical Education*. They had discovered Lloyd's three publications with Dr. Mabery in the *American Chemical Journal* while preparing their history of organic chemistry in the United States.

1982 October: Glenda Peterson publishes a story about Dr. Lloyd and the Tarbells' research in Lincoln's *Sunday Journal and Star*. Peterson begins with a list of all the ways Dr. Lloyd has been overlooked or forgotten with the sole exception of Manley's history of the University.

1994 and 1995: Mary Creese begins her decades-long project to document women chemists around the world. She publishes a succinct biography of Dr. Lloyd in *American Chemists and*

Chemical Engineers in 1994 and, with her husband, in the *Bulletin of the History of Chemistry* in 1995.

1997 October: Mark Griep prints the first version of his *The University of Nebraska's First Two Chemists: Hudson H. Nicholson and Rachel A. Holloway Lloyd* to distribute to his colleagues and visiting guests. The book has been continually updated and portions of it served as the basis for this *Easy and Lucid Guide*. Griep has given talks about Lloyd (and Nicholson) at a number of regional colleges, to the Nebraska ACS Local Section, at an ACS Midwest Regional meeting, and at two Biennial Conference on Chemical Education meetings.

1998: Marlene and Geoffrey Rayner-Canham publish *Women in Chemistry: Their Changing Roles from Alchemical Times to the Mid-Twentieth Century.* They have a section on Dr. Lloyd.

2000: The University of Nebraska-Lincoln places items on a webpage that describe the highlights of its history. The webpage includes several items prepared by me for chemistry's contribution including, "The first two women to become members of the American Chemical Society were Rachel Lloyd in 1891 and Rosa Bouton in 1893." I had come to this conclusion after reading Margaret W. Rossiter's *Women Scientists in America* (1982). She wrote that Rachel Bodley had been voted in along with the other honorary vice presidents of the meeting that led to the creation of ACS, which in my mind was a special case. I should have qualified my statement.

2001: The University of Nebraska webpage entry served as the focus of a series of entries in the Newscripts section of *Chemical and Engineering News* from May to July 2001. The first entry on May 7 was prompted by Mary Singleton of Pleasanton, California. She pointed out that Rachel Bodley was the first female member of ACS and not Rachel Lloyd. I felt this was a technicality so the second entry on June 11 was prompted by a letter from me. I cited Rossiter's book as the source for my statement but agreed I should have qualified my statement saying, "I accept that Bodley was the first woman ACS member as long as it is clarified that she was an honorary vice president [and thus did not join the society by the normal means]." The third and final Newscripts entry on July 9 was prompted by a letter from James Bohning at Lehigh University in Bethlehem, Pa. He writes, "You include information…that continues several misconceptions that have existed for many years." He points out that Bodley was among the 220 prominent chemists who received a formal letter of membership to create ACS in March 1876. Bodley accepted and, therefore, was the first regularly admitted female member. This means Rachel Lloyd was second and Rosa Bouton third.

2003: Sandra Singer publishes *Adventures Abroad* in which she describes the complex and overlapping paths that U.S. women took to earn the first math and science degrees in European universities. She documents that Dr. Lloyd was "the second woman to earn a doctorate in chemistry in Europe."

2012 October 19: Dr. Marinda Wu, President Elect of the American Chemical Society, visits the Chemistry Department at the University of Nebraska-Lincoln. During her visit, I tell her about Dr. Rachel Lloyd being the first U.S. woman to earn a Ph.D. in chemistry and the second female member of ACS. She urges me to apply for a National Historical Chemical Landmark. Since I am chair elect of the ACS Nebraska Local Section, I ask the Local Section Executive Board whether they would support me in this venture and they do. While preparing the nomination, I realize there is enough new material available to write this book.

2014 May 12: After 98 years, I was able to have the time capsule removed from the Avery Hall cornerstone. I was searching of a photo of Dr. Rachel Lloyd in anticipation of the National Historic Chemical Landmark celebration that ___ will take place in October 2014. The surprise is that a copy of Clement E. Lloyd's biography of Rachel Lloyd is in the capsule — the only known copy. A good quality photo of Dr. Lloyd is the frontispiece. The time capsule was a copper box about 15 in. x 15 in. x 10 in. that was soldered closed. About half the items in the capsule are related to Prof. Mary Fossler suggesting that she coordinated its assembly. Fossler earned her Chemistry B. Sc. from the Department in 1894. While she was an undergraduate, she worked as a Chemistry Laboratory Assistant for Dr. Rachel Lloyd. Fossler's three sisters also earned their degrees at the University of Nebraska: Christine in 1893; Anna in 1895; and Mabel in 1907. In fact, Mabel also majored in Chemistry. Fossler earned her Chemistry M. A. in 1898 while working under Dr. Samuel Avery in the area of organic synthesis; hers was the Department's thirteenth graduate degree. Upon graduation, she was hired as an Assistant Professor and then rose through the ranks. At least eight students earned their master's degrees under her direction between 1915 and 1919.

2014 October 1: The American Chemical Society confers National Historic Landmark status to "Dr. Rachel Lloyd and the Nebraska Beet Sugar Industry" at a banquet sponsored by the Nebraska ACS Local Section and the UNL Chemistry Department.

Rachel Lloyd Frontispiece from Clement Lloyd's 1901 Biography

In this image, it is possible to see her headband, earrings, necklace, neck bow, and dress pattern

The Robert Smith Holloway & Abigail Taber Family

The starting set of names and dates for the Lloyd family was from "Genealogy of the Holloway Families" by Olin E. Holloway, 1927, privately published in Knightstown, Indiana, and from "Encyclopedia of American Quaker Genealogy" compiled by T. W. Marshall, 1936, privately published in Ann Arbor, Michigan. Census records and other sources were then used to enhance the resulting outline.

Robert Smith Holloway

Robert is born April 8, 1807 in Stafford, Virginia, the son of Aaron Holloway (1779-1826) and Rachel Smith (1785-1840)

1825-1831: Robert Holloway is paying taxes in Flushing Township, Ohio

Robert married October 11, 1833 in New Bedford, Mass., to **Abigail Taber**

> The Flushing Meeting House Minutes of 11 October 1833 indicates that Robert Hathaway [*sic*] is granted a certificate to marry Abby Taber of the New Bedford Meeting House.

> Abigail is born December 13, 1809 in New Bedford, Massachusetts, the daughter of Francis Taber and Lydia.

1833: Robert S. Holloway privately publishes "Easy and Lucid Guide to a Knowledge of English Grammar." This book can be found in the U. S. Library of Congress, a dozen other libraries, and is now free online. Robert Holloway's motto appears to be "Language is the principal instrument of all intellectual knowledge."

EASY AND LUCID GUIDE

TO A KNOWLEDGE OF

ENGLISH GRAMMAR,

CONTAINING THE

PRINCIPLES AND RULES OF THE LANGUAGE,

CONFORMED TO THE BEST MODERN USAGES,

AND ILLUSTRATED BY APPROPRIATE AND INSTRUCTIVE EXAMPLES;

A Philosophic Exposition of the derivation and original meaning of words:

TO WHICH ARE ADDED,

A Key to False Syntax, and Punctuation;

AND

A NEW PARSING KEY,

In which the Parsing Lessons are, by means of Characters, briefly and comprehensively parsed:

ESPECIALLY DESIGNED FOR PRIVATE LEARNERS AND SCHOOLS.

BY ROBERT S. HOLLOWAY.

Language is the principal instrument of all intellectual knowledge.

St. Clairsville:

PRINTED FOR THE AUTHOR,

BY HORTON J. HOWARD.

1833.

Cover page from Robert S. Holloway's Grammar Textbook, 1833

This image is from Archive.org but it has been cleaned up using Adobe Photoshop.

1837: Robert and Abby were hired as two of the first four teachers at the new Mount Pleasant Boarding School

1838: Robert's ill health meant they had to resign their teaching posts

1840 Census: Smyrna, Ohio: Robert S Holloway

By 1843, Robert is working for the US Post Office in Smyrna, Ohio

Abby dies November 24, 1844 in Smyrna, Ohio. Abby is buried next to her three children (and later her husband) in the Guernsey Quaker Cemetery, one mile south of Smyrna next to where a Friends Church had been located. Smyrna is located in Harrison County but the Cemetery is located in Guernsey County.

Robert married 2nd May 2, 1849 to Deborah Smart
>   Deborah is born February 12, 1807 in New Jersey, the daughter (9th child) of Isaac Smart and Rebecca Thompson

1850 Census: Flushing, OH: Robert S Holloway 43, Deborah 43, Rachel A 11, and relative Alvirah 32

Robert died June 22, 1851, age 44. He is buried in Guernsey Quaker Cemetery, near his first wife. He did not leave a will and there is probate in either Harrison or Guernsey County.

Deborah Smart Holloway marries March 29, 1854 in Flushing to Jehu Fawcett, and becomes his third wife

1860 Census: Salem Perry Township, Ohio: Jehn Fawcett 57, Deborah 52, servant Martha Morwitz 18

Jehu (or Jehn) Fawcett dies February 8, 1867

1870 Census: Ohio: Deborah Fawcett 63 is living with the William Fisher family

Deborah Fawcett dies August 20, 1876 in Philadelphia. Her stepdaughter Rachel Lloyd is working at the Chestnut Female Seminary in Philadelphia at this time but it is not known whether they were living together.

Supposedly, Jehu's three wives are buried adjacent to one another in the Friends Cemetery on South Ellsworth St. in Salem, Ohio

Robert and Abigail's children:

1. Lydia T. Holloway
    born July 13, 1834; died February 13, 1836, age 1½

2. **Rachel Abbie Holloway Lloyd**
    born January 26, 1839 in Smyrna (or Flushing), Ohio
    married May 11, 1859 at St. Philip's Church to **Franklin C. Lloyd**
    >   Franklin born January 12, 1832 in Philadelphia
    children:
    1. Fanny L. Lloyd
        born October 27, 1860 in Philadelphia; died November 11, 1860 in Philadelphia
    2. William C. Lloyd
        born August 20, 1865 in Philadelphia; died October 7, 1865 in Philadelphia

3. Mary Holloway
    born February 19, 1841; died February 19, 1841; buried in Guernsey Quaker Cemetery

4. Francis Taber Holloway
    born April 29, 1842; died May 27, 1842; buried in Guernsey Quaker Cemetery

The Isaac Lloyd III and Hannah Scull Bolton Family

The starting set of names and dates for the Lloyd family was from "A Record of the descendants of Robert Lloyd who came from Wales and settled in The Welsh Tract at Merion Pennsylvania about 1684", compiled by R. Louis Lloyd, 1947, privately published. R. Louis Lloyd was the son of Clement E. Lloyd, whose family seemed to be closest to Rachel and Frank. Census records and other sources were then used to enhance the resulting outline.

Isaac Lloyd III
born September 22, 1800 in Philadelphia
married November 1, 1827 at Arch St. Friends' Meeting House, Phil. to **Hannah Scull Bolton**
      born September 8, 1807 in Philadelphia
      daughter of Samuel Bolton and Rachel Scull
1840 Census: need to search further
1850 Census: South Ward, Camden, NJ: Isaac Lloyd 50, Hannah 43, Elizabeth 22, Franklin 19, Horace 11, Clement 7, Fanny 0, and a servant
Hannah dies April 23, 1851 in Camden, NJ, age 43
Isaac married 2nd to Caroline W. Butcher
      born October 3, 1828 in Marlton, NJ
      died December 7, 1858, age 30
1860 Census: South Ward, Camden, NJ: Isaac Lloyd 59, Clement 17 b PA, Fanny 10 b PA, Morris 4 b NJ, Charles 1 b NJ, Sophia L Stiles 54, Mary Stiles 26
1860: Family moved back to Philadelphia about this time and lived at 824 Lombard Street
Merchant on Water Street; Secretary and Treasurer of Camden and Atlantic Land Co.
1870 Census: need to search further
Isaac dies May 13, 1876 in Philadelphia, age 75; buried in Woodlands Cemetery, Philadelphia

Isaac and Hannah's children:
1. **Elizabeth Scull Lloyd Orrick**
    born August 26, 1828 in Philadelphia
    married May 29, 1851 in Mary Bolton's home to **Newton Lane Orrick**
        born June 24, 1828 in Lancaster, PA
        died May 5, 1887 in Point Pleasant, NJ; buried at Woodlands Cemetery
      Newton was Secretary and Treasurer of The Pennsylvania Company for Insurance on Lives and Granting Annuities
    died November 5, 1912; buried at Woodlands Cemetery
    children:
    1. Caroline Ross Orrick
        born November 25, 1852 in Philadelphia
        died July 23, 1920; buried at Woodlands Cemetery
    2. Samuel Davenport Orrick
        born February 21, 1854 in Philadelphia
        died July 5, 1854 in Philadelphia, age 5 months; buried at Woodlands Cemetery
2. Bolton Lloyd

born March 10, 1830 in Philadelphia

died August 15, 1850 in Philadelphia, age 20

3. **Franklin C. Lloyd**

born January 12, 1832 in Philadelphia

married May 11, 1859 at St. Philip's Church to **Rachel Abbie Holloway**

   Rachel born January 26, 1839 in Smyrna (or Flushing), Ohio

died October 7, 1865 in Bangor (or Bay City), Michigan

children:

1. Fanny L. Lloyd

   born or October 27, 1860 in Philadelphia

   died November 11, 1860 in Philadelphia

2. William C. Lloyd

   born August 20, 1865 in Philadelphia

   died October 6 (or 7), 1865 in Philadelphia

4. **William C. Lloyd**

born August 12, 1833 in Philadelphia

married 1st October 6, 1857 at St. Philip's Church to **Elizabeth Hopper Rowlett**

   born October 6, 1838

   died February 15, 1900, age 61; buried at Woodlands Cemetery, Philadelphia

married 2nd September 24, 1902 in Ashville, NC, to Emily Bonneau Atkinson

   born September 24, 1868

   died January 5, 1935

died January 20, 1917; buried at Woodlands Cemetery, Philadelphia

William and Elizabeth's children:

1. Lucy Lloyd

   born August 12, 1858 in Philadelphia

   died August 16, 1858 in Philadelphia, 4 days old; buried at Woodlands Cemetery

2. Helen Lloyd

   born October 31, 1859 in Philadelphia

   died November 1, 1859 in Philadelphia, 2 days old; buried at Woodlands Cemetery

3. William C. Lloyd Jr.

   born March 1, 1865 in Philadelphia

   died December 3, 1881 in Philadelphia, age 16; buried at Woodlands Cemetery

4. Franklin Lloyd

   born August 14, 1866 in Philadelphia

   married Nathalie Churchman Lloyd, his second cousin

   they had one daughter

5. Lewis Lloyd

born June 18, 1838 in Philadelphia

died July 11, 1838 in Philadelphia, age one month

6. **Horace Lloyd**

born November 25, 1839 in Philadelphia

attended Westtown School

married 1st April 1865 in Phoenixville, PA to **Mary Eliza Vanderslice**

   born June 19, 1844 in Phoenixville

died January 9, 1881 in Phoenixville

1870 Census: Pennsylvania: Horace Lloyd 30, Mary E 27

1880 Census: Phoenixville PA: Horace Lloyd 39, Mary Eliza 37, Elizabeth 9, Carrie V. 7, and a servant

married 2nd September 19, 1882 in Phoenixville to Clara V. Jester

born November 1, 1857 in Uwchlan Township, Chester Co., PA

Bank teller in Phoenixville

1900 Census: Phoenixville PA: Horace Lloyd 61, Clara V 43, Elizabeth 30, Carrie V 28

Horace died October 13, 1911

Horace and Mary Eliza's children:

1. Mary Elizabeth Lloyd

born January 28, 1866 in Phoenixville

died September 17, 1869 in Phoenixville, age 3

2. Elizabeth Lloyd

born August 3, 1870 in Phoenixville

3. Carrie V. Lloyd

born September 26, 1872 in Phoenixville

7. Edwin Lloyd

born August 19, 1841 in Philadelphia

died August 30, 1842 in Philadelphia, age 1

8. **Clement E. Lloyd**

born March 24, 1843 in Philadelphia

1852-1858: Attended Westtown School in West Chester

married June 13, 1866 at St. Paul's Church to **Irene Emma Githens**

born August 17, 1843 in Philadelphia

died October 8, 1894

Clement died April 28, 1911 in Philadelphia, age 68

See the more complete description of his family in the next section

9. Fanny Lloyd

born September 1, 1850 in Camden, New Jersey

1859: entered Westtown School; contracted diphtheria at the end of her first school year

died July 1, 1860 of diphtheria in Philadelphia, age 9

Isaac and Caroline's children:

10. **Morris Lloyd**

born October 8, 1856 in Camden, New Jersey

married June 23, 1887 in Girard Ave Friends' Meeting House to **Annie Morgan Ambler**

born April 18, 1859 in Pennsylvania

died 1954

Journalist

1880 Census: Philadelphia: Morris Lloyd 23, is living with stepbrother Clement E Lloyd 37, Irene E 36, Clement E 11, R. Louis 10, Fanny 8, Morton G 5, and a servant

1900 Census: West Grove PA: Morris Lloyd 44, Annie M 41, Robert L 8, and a servant

1910 Census: Chambersburg PA: Morris Lloyd 53, Annie M 50, and Robert L 18

1920 Census: need to search further

1930 Census: Chambersburg PA: Morris Lloyd 73, Annie M 70
Morris died March 23, 1932
child:
1. Robert Lowery Lloyd
        born February 14, 1892 in Philadelphia
        married June 21, 1930 in New York City to Josephine Jewett
                born June 6, 1900
        Robert died 1986
            they had one child
11. Charles Lloyd
    born November 28, 1858 in Camden, New Jersey
    died September 17, 1876 in Atlantic City, NJ, age 17
    buried in Woodlands Cemetery, Philadelphia

The Clement Lloyd and Irene Gibbens Family

Clement Ernest Lloyd
born March 24, 1843 in Philadelphia
His mother died in 1851 when he was 8 years old
1852-1858: Attended Westtown School in West Chester
married June 13, 1866 at St. Paul's Church, Philadelphia to **Irene Emma Gibbens**
> born August 17, 1843 in Philadelphia
> daughter of William Morton Gibbens and Jane Sterling
> Irene died October 8, 1894

1866-1902: lived in Beverly, New Jersey, 15 miles from Philadelphia
1870 Census: New Jersey: Clement Lloyd 27, Irene 26, Clement 2, Richard 0, John Lloyd 22 cousin?, and a servant
1880 Census: Philadelphia: Clement E Lloyd 37, Irene E 36, Clement E 11, R. Louis 10, Fanny 8, Morton G 5 Morris Lloyd 23 stepbrother, and a servant
1900 Census: need to search further
1901: Privately published a memorial of Dr. Rachel Lloyd, his sister-in-law. The only existing copy was found in the Avery Hall time capsule on the University of Nebraska-Lincoln campus in May 2014.
1903: living at 400 Chestnut Street
Clement died April 28, 1911 in Philadelphia
Clement buried at Woodlands Cemetery, Philadelphia (after cremation)
children:

1. **Clement Ernest Lloyd Jr.**
   born August 11, 1868 in Delanco, New Jersey
   married 1st September 17, 1894 in Cleveland, Ohio, to **Maude A. Denzer**
   > born December 16, 1871 in Cleveland
   > daughter of Charles H. Denzer and Josephine Pere
   > died April 30, 1895 in Landsdowne, Pennsylvania

Clement E. Lloyd, Jr., 1890
Photo from the Temple University Archives.

Clement E. Lloyd, Jr., 1894
Photo from the Temple University Archives.

1897-99: Attended Temple University
married 2nd November 9, 1899 in Philadelphia to May C. Hansell
> born May 24, 1878 in Philadelphia
> daughter of Davis H. Hansell and Mary Steele Holmes

Lumber merchant in Philadelphia, working out of the Girard Trust Building
> *1900 Census: need to search further*
> 1910 Census: Philadelphia Ward 42: Clement E Lloyd Jr 37, May C 31, Robert H 8, and David H Hansell 65 father-in-law
> 1920 Census: Philadelphia Ward 42: C E Lloyd Jr 51, M L 41, R H 18, and two servants

child:
1. Robert Harold Lloyd
> born January 3, 1902 in Philadelphia
> married 1927 in Philadelphia to Margaret S. Leitch
>> died August 1, 1994 in Honolulu
>>> Robert and Margaret had two children. I contacted one of them in 2014, who said his family lost touch with the Lloyd side long ago and they didn't inherit any items of historical interest from them.

2. **Richard Louis Lloyd**
born February 6, 1870 in Beverly, New Jersey; he was known as R. Louis Lloyd
At Central High School, he earned an A.M.
Philadelphia College of Pharmacy, where he earned a Ph.G. [*Graduate of Pharmacy*]
married March 23, 1897 at Race St. Meeting House to **Margaret Mercy Powell**
> born November 30, 1875 in Philadelphia
> daughter of Abram G. Powell and Sarah E. Williamson

After marriage, they moved to Rochester, NY where he entered the drug retail business for less than three years
1900 February: returned to Philadelphia where he obtained job at Philadelphia Electric Co.; they lived at 3206 Sumner St.
1944: privately published *Poems by R. Louis Lloyd, written for various occasions since the author was 21 years of age.* Copies of this are in the libraries of Haverford College and Swarthmore College.
1947: privately published *A record of the descendants of Robert Lloyd who came from Wales and settled in the Welsh tract at Merion, Pennsylvania, about 1684* by R. Louis Lloyd. This book is widely available. I used it to begin assembling this family history and then used census records to extend it a generation further.
1947: R. Louis Lloyd donated papers to Swarthmore College, which lists "An Inventory of the Lloyd Family Papers, 1769-1890" that "descended in the family" including "Some notes in handwriting of Clement E. Lloyd." The archivist says there is nothing about Rachel Lloyd in these papers but she did send the 1865 obituary about Franklin Lloyd that is signed R*.
died October 13, 1949 in West Chester, Pennsylvania
children:
1. Passmore Williamson Lloyd
> born December 24, 1897 in Rochester
> married to Estelle, same age
> 1930 Census: living in New Castle, NJ
> 1940 Census: living in Rochester, NY
> they had four children but I could not trace them past their births
2. Dorothy Lloyd
> born June 30, 1899 in in Rochester ___

3. Beulah Clement Lloyd
    born December 9, 1901 in Philadelphia
3. **Fanny Lloyd Maginniss**
    born February 24, 1872 in Beverly, New Jersey
    married November 24, 1897 at St. John's Church to **Thomas Hobbs Maginniss, Jr.**
        born August 16, 1876 in Fort McHenry, Maryland
        son of Col. Thomas Hobbs Maginniss and Sarah Thompson
        educated at St. John's Military Academy, Haddonheld, NJ
        1894-1895: Student of Law
        1896-1899: University of Pennsylvania, Clerk in Secretary's Office
        1900-1910: International Text-Book Co. in Scranton, PA, department manager
        1910-?: West Philadelphia Real Estate Company
        1913: Thomas wrote *The Irish Contribution to America's Independence*, Doire Publ.,
            Philadelphia
        Thomas died September 15, 1944 in Larchmont, PA
    Fanny died January 26, 1958; buried in Arlington Cemetery, Drexel Hill, PA
    children:
    1. Kathleen Maginnis
        born December 4, 1898 in Scranton
        Attended Pennsylvania State Normal School
    2. Irene Emma Maginnis
        born July 8, 1900 in Scranton
        1921 B.A., Bryn Mawr College
    3. Hamilton John Maginnis
        born September 3, 1906 in Scranton
        married to Elizabeth Pedlow
            born December 12, 1907 in New York
            died March 3, 1993 in Florida
        died February 27, 1977 in Mansfield, Ohio
    4. Lloyd Maginnis
        born ?
4. **Morton Githens Lloyd**
    born September 10, 1874 in Beverly, New Jersey
    1896 electrical engineering degree from University of Pennsylvania
    married to **Ethel T.**
    worked at the Bureau of Standards and published seven technical papers
    1940 Census, living with wife in Montgomery MD
    died 1941

News Articles, Book Extracts, Brochures, & Letters

Public Ledger (Philadelphia)
Wednesday, July 10, 1844, p. 2

Franklin Lloyd admitted to Central High School

Central High School.—A list of pupils admitted to the Central High School, July 5th, 1844:—[*90 students, including*] Franklin Lloyd

---

"Chestnut Street Female Seminary"
1850 Prospectus

[*This is the inaugural prospectus when their street address was 525 Chestnut. Later renumbering by the city changed it to 1615 Chestnut. Rachel Lloyd taught here from 1873 to 1880, after they had been in operation for two decades.*]

Chestnut St. Female Seminary, 1850 Prospectus

Title Page

CHESTNUT STREET

FEMALE SEMINARY,

NO. 525 CHESTNUT STREET
PHILADELPHIA.

Philadelphia:
Printed by John Young, Black Horse Alley.
1850

Page 3
CHESTNUT STREET
FEMALE SEMINARY,
PHILADELPHIA.

Associate Principals.
Mary L. Bonney,
Harriette A. Dillaye.

Miss Bonney, late of Miss Philips' School,
    Walnut Street, Philadelphia, and
Miss Dillaye, for the last five years of the Troy
    Female Seminary.

Will Open A
BOARDING AND DAY SCHOOL,
The 1st of September next,
at 525 Chestnut Street.

Page 3
The Course of Study

Will include all branches constituting a thorough scientific and literary education. The primary object will be to elicit and strengthen the intellectual powers, refine the taste and cultivate the heart. A solid foundation in the elementary branches will be considered indispensable to the subsequent intellectual structure.

Knowing that the proper cultivation of the moral and social parts of our nature is intimately connected with usefulness and happiness, no less care will be taken in their development than in the cultivation of the mind and manners.

Misses Bonney and Dillaye have been so fortunate as to secure for the Music Department Professor Gustave Blessner and Lady, formerly of this City and late of Troy Female Seminary, Artists whose composition and execution, combined with their long and successful experience as teachers, offer inducements of no ordinary character to those who would excel in the science as well as the art of music.

The Department of Penciling, Crayon and Painting in Oil and Water Colors, will be under the care of an able teacher.

Miss Dillaye will have the superintendence of the French Department. Her father being a native of France she has been familiar with the French accent from childhood; having availed herself of the ablest masters of the language, and having years of experience in teaching it, Miss Dillaye assumes the responsibility of securing to that department, through herself and masters, all the facilities necessary to a thorough acquaintance of the language.

The Scholastic year will commence the First of September, and close the last of June. The year will be divided into two Sessions. The full explanation of the first few weeks of a Session and reviews of the last, are considered so essential that no deduction will be made for absences at either of these periods, except for illness; indeed, no deduction, except for illness, will be made for absence at *any time.*

Great care will be taken of the health of the young ladies.

The number of Boarding Pupils will be limited to Twenty.

TERMS FOR BOARDERS:

Board and washing, with Tuition in the English Branches and French, $300 per annum.

Music, Painting, Drawing and Foreign Languages (except French) at Professors' charges.

Use of Piano per Session, $6.00. Harp, $10.00. Guitar, $2.00.

Each Boarder will supply herself with table and toilet napkins, silver fork and spoons.

Pew rent at cost.

If Parents desire clothing furnished, money must be advanced to meet the expense.

TUITION PAYABLE QUARTERLY IN
    ADVANCE.

TERMS FOR DAY-SCHOLARS:

Senior Class—Tuition in Eng. & French, $50 per Session
Junior   "   "   "   "   40
Primary "   Under 12 years of age,   30
No Pupil admitted for less than one Session

TESTIMONIALS:

Miss Bonney and Miss Dillaye are Teachers of uncommon ability and faithfulness. This I know from personal observation.

    Emma   Willard,   Troy
        Female Seminary, June
        10, 1850.

[*The reference includes 9 Rev., 3 Esq., 2 Hon., 2 Mrs., 1 Prof., and 1 Dr.*]

"Philadelphia As It Is" by R. A. Smith, 1852, Philadelphia: Lindsay and Blakiston, p. 130

POWERS & WEIGHTMAN [*Ad*]

Public Ledger (Philadelphia)
Wednesday, April 21, 1852, p. 3

WANTED—One or two good STONE MASONS. Apply at FRANKLIN LLOYD'S Store, near Darby.

Philadelphia Inquirer
May 12, 1859

MARRIED.

On the morning of 11th instant, in St. Philip's Church, by Rev. O. D. Cooper, FRANKLIN LLOYD to RACHEL A. HOLLOWAY, daughter of the late Robert S. Holloway, of Flushing, Ohio.

Philadelphia Inquirer
Thursday, September 26, 1861, p. 8
[*This undertaker handled the most of the Lloyds who were buried in Woodlands Cemetery, including Frank*]

[Undertaker's Advertisement]

Wm. Hill Moore, Furnishing undertaker, at his old stand, 505 Arch street, about Fifth. Metallic Coffins constantly on hand. Particular attention paid to persons desirous of purchasing grounds in Woodlands Cemetery.

Chestnut St. Female Seminary, 1862 Brochure

Title Page

CHESTNUT STREET

FEMALE SEMINARY,

Boarding and Day School,
NO. 1615 CHESTNUT STREET.

_____

Principals,
Mary L. Bonney, Harriette A. Dillaye.

_____

Philadelphia:
Henry B. Ashmead, Book and Job Printer,
Nos. 1102 and 1104 Sansom Street.
1862

Page 3 [*The following enhances the 1850 Prospectus*]
The Course of Study

This Seminary, opened in 1850, is pleasantly situated in the upper part of Chestnut Street—a location combining all the advantages of this city, with comparative retirement. The house is commodious and pleasant, and no expense has been spared to make it attractive and homelike.

[*Paragraph similar to 1850 brochure is omitted.*]

To one feature of the Boarding School special attention is solicited. Three evenings in the week, the teachers and pupils meet for reading. Each member of the family takes her turn alphabetically as reader, while the other members of the group are engaged in any work that taste may suggest. These readings subserve important purposes. They call the school together as a family, enlarge general knowledge—necessarily very limited while the attention is so exclusively confined to text-books—induce a taste for systematic reading, and cultivate the *attention* by requiring a brief analysis of the subject, when completed.

History, with current literature and events, receives special attention in these readings.

[*Paragraph similar to 1850 brochure is omitted.*]

Diplomas are given to pupils, in both departments, who have passed the Senior Examination in a manner satisfactory to the Principals.

Much care is taken to secure to the pupils the varied advantages of this large city. Lectures—historical, scientific and literary—facilitating their regular studies, and adding to their general information upon subjects not included in the course, are selected with great care.

Pupils in Music are furnished with every facility for cultivating their taste by hearing the best artists that visit the city.

All objects of general or local interest in the vicinity are visited, and each in turn becomes a subject for descriptive writing.

Great care is taken of the *health* of the young ladies. Thorough ventilation, bathing, calisthenics, and active exercise in the open air, are among daily school duties. Excursions into the surrounding country are frequent.

To secure the highest improvement, physical, mental and moral, of those confided to our care, is *the* object of our efforts.

_____

Text Books: [*List of math & science books.*]
Junior Class.

Emerson's Second Part to Fractions; Warren's Primary Geography; Swift's Natural Philosophy; Hooker's Book of Nature; Stoddard's Juvenile Mental Arithmetic

Middle Class.

Mitchell's Geography; Ancient Geography; Emerson's Arithmetic continued; Phelps' Natural Philosophy; Familiar Sciences; Smellie's Philosophy of Natural History.

Senior Class.

Davies' Arithmetic; Davies' Algebra and Geometry; Cutter's Physiology; Wood's Botany; Geology; Burritt's Geography of the Heavens, with Mattison's Astronomy and Maps; *Youmans' Chemistry [Italics added]*; Beecher's Domestic Economy; Wayland's Moral Science; Bible with Coleman's Biblical Geography

The above list of Text Books are those now used in the classes. To avoid unnecessary expenses to the patrons, changes will be made from time to time, only when by so doing the best interests of the scholars are advanced.

[*Edward L. Youmans and his sister Eliza Ann Youmans wrote several science books together. Eliza Ann also wrote botany books. As Edward was losing his eyesight in 1845, they embarked on a study of physics and chemistry in which Eliza would read to him and perform experiments while describing the results. In 1851, they studied agricultural chemistry, which prompted him to suggest they write "A Class-Book of Chemistry." It was clearly written and sold many copies. In 1872, Edward, Eliza Ann, and their other brother founded "Popular Science Monthly" that remains the most highly subscribed science magazine.]*

"Return of a Death in the City of Philadelphia, Physician's Certificate" November 16, 1860

Fannie Lloyd's Death Certificate

1. Name of Deceased,	Fannie Lloyd
2. Colour,	White
3. Sex,	Female
4. Age,	19 days
5. Married or Single,	Single
6. Date of Death,	November 15th, 1860
7. Cause of Death,	Disease of the Brain
W. Williamson, M.D.	
Residence, N.E. cor. 11th & Filbert St.	
8. Occupation,	
9. Place of Birth,	Philad[a]
10. When a minor,	
Name of Father,	Franklin Lloyd
Name of Mother,	Rachel Lloyd
11. Ward,	13th
12. Street and Number,	Green St. No. 731
13. Date of Burial,	16th Nov 1860
14. Place of Burial,	Woodlands Cemeter
Robt. R. Brighurst, UNDERTAKER	
Residence, No. 38 North 11th St.	

"Return of a Death in the City of Philadelphia, Physician's Certificate" October 13, 1865

William C. Lloyd's Death Certificate

1. Name of Deceased,	William C. Lloyd
2. Colour,	White
3. Sex,	Male
4. Age,	1 mo, 20 dys
5. Married or Single,	Single
6. Date of Death,	Oct. 7, 1865
7. Cause of Death,	Jaundice
W. H. Williamson, M.D.	
Residence, N.E. cor. 11th & Filbert St.	
8. Occupation,	
9. Place of Birth,	Phil.
10. When a minor,	
Name of Father,	Franklin Lloyd
Name of Mother,	
11. Ward,	6th
12. Street and Number,	505 Arch St.
13. Date of Burial,	Oct 13, 1865
14. Place of Burial,	Woodlands
Wm H Moore, UNDERTAKER	
Residence, 505 Arch St.	

"Return of a Death in the City of Philadelphia, Physician's Certificate" October 18, 1865

Franklin Lloyd's Death Certificate

1. Name of Deceased,	Franklin Lloyd
2. Colour,	White
3. Sex,	Male
4. Age,	33 yrs & 9 mos
5. Married or Single,	Married
6. Date of Death,	Oct. 7, 1865
7. Cause of Death,	Bilious Fever
W. H. Williamson, M.D.	
Residence, N.E. cor. 11th & Filbert St.	
8. Occupation,	[M?]
9. Place of Birth,	Phil.
10. When a minor,	
Name of Father,	
Name of Mother,	
11. Ward,	Bangor, Michigan
12. Street and Number,	
13. Date of Burial,	October 18, 1865
14. Place of Burial,	Woodlands
Wm H Moore, UNDERTAKER	
Residence, 505 Arch	

North American and United States Gazette (Phil.)
October 9 1865

𝕯eaths.

LLOYD.—At Bangor, Michigan, on the 6th inst., of congestion of the lungs. FRANKLIN LLOYD, in the 34th year of his age. Due notice will be given of the funeral.

Philadelphia Inquirer
October 13, 1865

DEATHS.

LLOYD.—On the 6th instant, at Bangor, Michigan, of congestion of the lungs, FRANKLIN LLOYD, in the 34th year of his age.

The relatives and friends of the family are respectfully invited to meet at Wm. H. Moore's, No. 505 Arch street, this day, 13th instant, at 10 o'clock. Interment at Woodlands Cemetery.

Unknown paper (probably Philadelphia)
October 1865 [*From Swarthmore College Archives*]

OBITUARY.

At Bangor, Michigan, on the 6th inst., FRANKLIN LLOYD, formerly of Philadelphia, in the 34th year of his age.

The dread archer has chosen a shining mark. He has added another to the list of his noble victims. To our short-sighted human vision, every circumstance conspires to make this bereavement more cruel, and our grief more poignant. A mind singularly gifted with those qualities which command the admiration of men, and tempered by that training in the school of Christ which makes them the blessing of society, might seem fitly to demand long years of usefulness. A judgment so clear and just, an integrity so unflinching, heart so generous and tender, an energy so untiring, would appear entitled, in the economy of human progress, to the fullest scope for their benign influence on the world. But "God seeth not as man seeth," and we record, submissively, our sorrow for one of the truest of men.

Every relation of life bears him grateful witness. As a son and brother, always thoughtful and affectionate, as a friend, of well tried and never failing constancy. And as a husband, the tenderness with which his first vows were breathed seemed to be only deepened and ripened by the lapse of time. At a sacrifice of self, he chose deliberately that position, in a comparatively unbroken country, which afforded the largest field for his industry and talent. With undaunted resolution, he met and conquered every difficulty of a new and untried enterprise, and at an age when the names of most men are scarcely heard in an active community, this young stranger was acknowledge and respected as a leading spirit. With a Christianity rather of words and deeds, his earliest care was to introduce among the rough elements of a new settlement the moulding institutions of the gospel. His own efforts established and maintained the Sabbath School and the preaching of the word found in him its zealous supporter. The tearful tribute of that community, after two years' acquaintance, claiming to mingle in the grief of his life-long friends, has in it an eloquence of testimony which heroes might envy.   R*

[*R* is a close family friend according to Clement Lloyd. It is not Rachel.*]

New York Times
April 27, 1871, page 2

Continental Travel

Today a large number leave for Liverpool by the *Adriatic*, the *City of Paris*, and the *Italy*.

By the steam-ship *City of Paris.*—
[*many names omitted*] Mrs. Rachel Lloyd.

Fort Wayne Daily Gazette (Indiana)
July 26, 1882, page 4

[New Principal at Foster School]

Miss Ada L. Howard has resigned as president of Wellesley college, Mass., and has accepted a position as lady principal of the Foster School at Clifton Springs, New York.

Courier-Journal (Louisville, Kentucky)
Wednesday, November 15, 1882, page 5

EDUCATIONAL.

Mrs. RACHEL LLOYD

Formerly Teacher of Chemistry in Philadelphia, more recently Lady Principal of the Foster school, New York, who for several summers has been engaged in original investigations in Chemical Science in Harvard University, Cambridge, Mass., now Instructor in Physics and Chemistry in Hampton College, has formed classes for experimental work in General Chemistry, Qualitative and Quantitative Analysis.

Persons desiring to join such classes will please make application at the College, 316 West Walnut street.

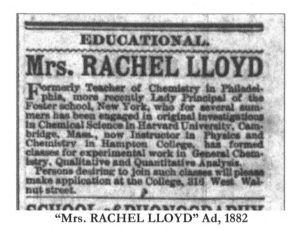

"Mrs. RACHEL LLOYD" Ad, 1882

New York Daily Tribune
Thursday, September 27, 1883, p. 1, c. 5

[School of Pharmacy for Women]

On the first Monday in October, a School of Pharmacy for women, a unique institution in this country, will open its doors in Louisville, Ky. Miss Kate Palmer is to be the botanist of the school and Mrs. Rachel Lloyd the chemist, but all the other instructors will be men. The promoters of this enterprise believe that women are specially qualified for the operations of the pharmacy, and that in training them for a new field of work a public benefit is conferred. It remains to be seen whether or not women will easily overcome the tendency, which cook books exemplify, to inaccuracy to numbers and quantities. "A teacupful of flour" or "a little salt," the recipe generally says, and experts rely upon some subtle sense and a mysterious faculty for compounding to make the product what it ought to be. But when it comes to prussic acid, accuracy is better than genius.

Bangor Daily Whig & Courier (Bangor, Maine)
Saturday, September 29, 1883, p. 1, c. 1
[*Note that only the supportive first half of the NY Daily Tribune article was reproduced in this newspaper.*]

[School of Pharmacy for Women]

On the first Monday in October, a School of Pharmacy for women, a unique institution in this country, will open its doors in Louisville, Ky. Miss Kate Palmer is to be the botanist of the school and Mrs. Rachel Lloyd the chemist, but all the other instructors will be men. The promoters of this enterprise believe that women are specially qualified for the operations of the pharmacy, and that in training them for a new field of work a public benefit is conferred.

"Louisville School of Pharmacy for Women."
Catalog, Louisville, Ky., 1883-4
[*From the University of Kentucky Archives*]

Louisville School of Pharmacy for Women.

[p. 5] **FACULTY.**

J. P. BARNUM, M. D.,
Professor of Pharmaceutical and Analytical Chemistry
DEAN OF THE FACULTY

VINCENT DAVIS, M. D.,
Professor of Theory and Practice of Pharmacy

MRS. RACHEL LLOYD,
Professor of Chemistry
SECRETARY OF THE FACULTY

P. F. SMITH,
Professor of Materia Medica

T. HUNT STUCKY, M. D.,
Professor of Microscopy

MISS KATE PALMER,
Professor of Botany

[p. 10] The Course in Chemistry.
by PROFESSOR LLOYD.

Junior Course.—Lectures on Sound, Heat, Light, Magentism, and Electricity, both frictional and dynamical. The remaining lectures of the junior course will be upon the metals and non-metals and their important compounds.

Senior Course.—Lectures upon the chemistry of carbon compounds, volumetric determinations, and Spectrum Analysis.

Both courses will be made thoroughly experimental.

Books recommended for reference—Attfield's Chemistry, Fowne's Chemistry, Sutton's Volumetric Analysis, Remsen's Wohler's Organic Chemistry (American Edition), Treatise on Chemistry, Roscoe and Schorlemmer.

"The Course in Chemistry" by Prof. Lloyd, 1883, at the Louisville School of Pharmacy for Women

[p. 15] Historical Sketch of the School.

The School of Pharmacy for Women had its origin in a demand for some especial educational facilities, by certain women already engaged in the business of the druggist, and also by others desiring to enter upon the same.

The demand appeared to the founders to prove first, that existing schools were not suitable for the especial needs of women, and secondly that the commercial value of women as chemists and druggists was beginning to be felt. In other words, the economic principle that whatever is good or efficient for any department of labor, should be utilized for the benefit of that department, has carried weight in determining this enterprise.

There are several reasons why existing schools are not altogether suitable for women. Prime among these is the deficiency of laboratory work in the college itself, the custom being to depend upon an apprenticeship during a stated number of years, under an established chemist and pharmacist, who is acting-preceptor for the time being. The work done under such a provision must be more or less variable, dependent as it would be upon the character of the preceptor the individual would be able to secure. But whatever may be the value of this method, it is at present practically closed to young women, and will continue to be so until woman as druggist is generally recognized.

To take the place of this apprenticeship, the especial feature of our School will be the full and extensive course in laboratory work. It is proposed to provide facilities for each pupil to work in Chemistry and Pharmacy through ten months of the year. In connection with the laboratory a chair is created, filled by a Professor whose duties as practical Pharmacist and Chemist, while corresponding in a certain sense to those of the so-called preceptor, will have the especial advantage of following a fixed schedule, sufficiently extensive to cover all compounds, etc., of the Pharmacist and Chemist, and at the same time systematic and exact, to meet the requirements of a disciplined college course. It is expected by this means to ensure proficiency in *all* cases.

To the regular course in this department will be added a supplemental course in the manufacture of chemicals and pharmaceuticals, usually purchased by the apothecary, and prepared in the laboratory of the manufacturing chemist only.

The chairs of Botany and Microscopy provide laboratory work peculiar to those departments.

To meet the pressing demand for immediate instruction, a Spring course was opened, and although some weeks in operation before any public announcement was made, a class was formed, encouraging in its size, mental caliber, and zeal for the work.

Since our purpose has been made public, flattering notices have appeared through the press, in various parts of the country. At this present time, we have had direct application for information from nineteen of the United States and from Canada. We are led by these indications to believe that the College of Pharmacy for Women opened at a period ripe for such an enterprise. Should this be the case, its success is assured.

The following are the names of those in attendance during the first session:

Miss Fay Barnum,   Miss C. Belle Papin,
Miss Lucy S. Beasley,   Miss Florence Shafer,
Mrs. W. L. Buzan,   Miss Margie Shafer,
Miss Jennie Cochran,   Miss Fauntine Vetter,
Miss Hope Ghiselin,   Mrs. E. J. Wightman,
Mrs. Anne Blades Irvine, Miss Florence Wightman,
Miss Mary Jarvis,   Mr. Herbert McConnethy,*
        Mr. Dwight H. Marble.*

---

*While the school was opened for the education of women, and male students are not solicited, the above named gentlemen were received into the class by permission of the Faculty.

American Chemical Journal
Volume 6, pp. 157-165 (1884)

XLI.—On α- and β-chlordibromacrylic acids[1]

by CHARLES F. MABERY AND RACHEL LLOYD

Footnote 1: The results described in papers XLI, XLII, and XLIII were obtained under my direction in the summer of instruction in chemistry for 1883.—C.F.M.

In a former paper by F. C. Robinson and one of us, a brief account was given of certain experiments in which we had tried to obtain an addition product of brompropiolic acid with chlorine monobromide. Although the results then obtained were rather unsatisfactory, it seemed possible nevertheless to prepare the addition product in a state of purity, and this became especially desirable when it was found that an acid of the same empirical composition could be formed from chlortribrompriopionic acid.

A Brief History of Westtown Boarding School with a General Catalogue of Officers, Students, etc. by Watson W. Dewees, Third Edition, Philadelphia, 1884

A List of Students at Westtown School from 1799 to 1822

WESTTOWN BOARDING SCHOOL,
CHESTER COUNTY, PA.

Westtown Boarding School, 1884

FEMALES [starting page 223]

Fifth Thousand
Name. Residence. Date of Entry.
[page 316]
473. Rachel A. Holloway, Flushing, Ohio, 10th mo., 1853

Passport issued May 14, 1885

Rachel Lloyd's 1885 Passport

Los Angeles Times
Tuesday, July 12, 1887, p. 1, c. 2

[Mrs. Rachel Lloyd Hired at University of Nebraska]

Mrs. Rachel Lloyd has been appointed assistant professor of chemistry of the Nebraska State University for the coming year, at a salary of $1500. [*She earned an additional $500 per year as assistant chemist at the Agricultural Experiment Station.*]

The Atchison Daily Globe (Atchison, Kansas)
Saturday, July 23, 1887, p. 2, c. 7

[Mrs. Rachel Lloyd Hired at University of Nebraska]

Mrs. Rachel Lloyd makes $1500 a year teaching chemistry to students of the Nebraska state university.

Woman's Tribune
August 1887

Professor Rachel Lloyd.

The faculty and students and all friends of the University of Nebraska are to be congratulated upon the election of Professor Rachel Lloyd, of Philadelphia, as Associate Professor of Chemistry. She is an exemplary Christian woman, of liberal education, and most refined manners, while her attainments in chemistry are of the highest order.

While at Harvard University prosecuting her chemical studies, she devoted several sessions to organic chemistry and subjects of original investigation, the results of which have been published in the American, English, German and French journals of chemistry. During an extended and successful experience in teaching physical science, Prof. Lloyd has occupied several prominent positions, the last of which was the Professorship of Chemistry at Hampton College, Louisville, Ky. In 1885 she obtained leave of absence from the latter position to take a course of study at the University of Zurich, Switzerland, where she recently received a doctorate degree, an honor that has been conferred in but few instances on American women. Her inaugural dissertation for the degree of Doctor of Philosophy, entitled, "On the Conversion of some of the Homologues of Benzol-Phenol into primary and secondary Amines," which was approved by the Philosophical Faculty of the University of Zurich and published in February 1887, is highly valued in chemical circles.

Dr. H. H. Nicholson, the Professor of Chemistry with whom Prof. Lloyd will be associated, ranks as one of the best chemists and most successful teachers in the country. It may be expected that these Professors will build up in the University of Nebraska a department of Chemistry that will compare favorably in scope and thoroughness of its work with the best Laboratories of the east.

Ada C. Bittenbender.

[*"Woman's Tribune" was a woman's suffrage magazine published in Beatrice, Nebraska, by Clara Bewick Colby from 1883 to 1902. Ada C. Bittenbender and her husband were both lawyers who moved to Lincoln, Nebraska, in 1882. She was one of the first women lawyers in Nebraska and the third woman admitted to practice before the Supreme Court. She argued cases in both state and federal courts and was active in the Woman's Christian Temperance Union and Woman's Suffrage movements.*]

Science, volume 10, pp. 82-84
August 12, 1887

Chemical Laboratory of the University of Nebraska

So many requests for the plans and a description of the new chemical laboratory of the University of Nebraska have been received since its erection, as to warrant the belief that a brief description of its general features would be of interest to the readers of *Science*, and especially to those who are contemplating similar buildings, or who are interested in the educational growth of the West.

The building is situated on the south-east corner of the university campus, fronting south on R Street. A wide street bounds the east side, while on the north and west is the open campus: thus the building commands an abundance of light from all directions.

Fig. 1 shows the south front and east side. The building consists of a high basement of native limestone, and a two-story super-structure of the finest St. Louis pressed brick, laid in black mortar and relieved by belt courses of rough limestone. The style of architecture is Romanesque, the broad and heavy stone arches and pointed towers giving to the whole an appearance of massiveness and solidity in keeping with its construction.

Chemical Laboratory, East Face, 1887

The entrances are in the south and north ends of the building; that in the south being the main one, while the north door is for the convenience of students coming to the laboratories from the other university buildings. Through this access is had to every work-room in the laboratory, and to the main lecture-room on the second floor. This arrangement brings classes into the lecture-room from the rear,—an arrangement that will be appreciated by every lecturer on experimental science.

Entering at the south door, we find ourselves in the vestibule of the first floor. At our right and left, stairways lead to the basement floor, as shown in Fig. 3. Descending to the basement corridor (Fig. 2), at the front is a large vestibule opening by double side-doors into an area where heavy material is received. Under the stairway to our right is a small room containing the gas-meter. Under the left-hand stairway, and extending across the space occupied by the vestibule, is a ladies' toilet-room. Immediately in front of the stairway is the elevator shaft. The room at the right serves as a store-room for the basement laboratories, and as a balance-room for the assay and metallurgical laboratory. The

corresponding room on the opposite side of the corridor contains a small upright boiler for furnishing distilled water, and large storage-tanks for hydrogen and oxygen gases. It serves also as a storage-room for acids and as a work-shop. The remaining portion of this floor is taken up by the general laboratory, where students beginning the study of chemistry do their work. This can be used as one large laboratory, accommodating seventy-five students at one time, or, by closing the communicating doors, be divided into two, A and B, A being used as an assay and metallurgical laboratory.

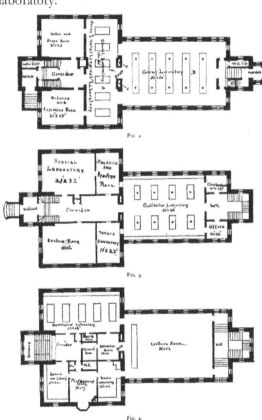

Chemical Laboratory Floor Plans, 1887

These rooms have high ceilings, and are well supplied with light. They are ventilated by means of the two large flues C and D, each of which is eight feet broad, and a series of smaller flues built into the side-walls, one between each pair of windows. The large flues open directly into the air; the smaller ones, into the space under the roof, which communicates with the air by means of the small, ventilating-tower on the rear part of the roof. On each floor, built into the space between the large flues, and opening into them, are large hoods accessible from both sides through sliding glass doors.

Extending along the side-walls—and this is the case in every laboratory-room in the building—is a table, furnished with gas and water, drawers and cupboards. These tables carry the smaller hoods, covering the sand and steam baths, and opening into the small flues. Space is also afforded here for such operations as require more room than the ordinary work-table gives.

Passing through the general laboratory, and ascending the stairway at the north end, we find ourselves in the north hall of the second floor (Fig. 3). On our right is a small room for blast-lamps and combustions. On the opposite side of the hall is the office and study of the associate professor of chemistry [*Prof. Lloyd's office*].

Passing on, we enter the qualitative laboratory. This is intended for the use of those students who have had some preliminary training, and has accommodations for thirty-two workers. Opening from this laboratory at the opposite corners are two rooms equal in size,—the one a balance and apparatus room; the other the private laboratory of the associate professor [*Prof. Lloyd's lab room*]. Beyond these, on opposite sides of the south corridor, are a small lecture-room and a special laboratory. In this laboratory the chemical work of the investigations undertaken by the experiment-station will be carried on [*students will do beet sugar analysis*].

Ascending the stairway at the end of the corridor, we reach the corridor of the second floor (Fig. 4). At our left is the quantitative laboratory, with accommodations for twenty students. Communicating with it is a small dark room for the storage of standard solutions.

Passing through the door in the north end of the room, we enter the main lecture-room. This room has a raised roof, placed at such a pitch that the top of the lecture-table can be seen from all parts of the room. It is furnished with Andrew's patent lecture-chair, and will comfortably seat two hundred people.

The lecture-table is large and roomy, and is abundantly supplied with water and gas. It is ventilated by powerful down draughts and movable box-hoods. Directly back of the table, and opening into the preparation-room, is one of the large hoods before mentioned. Connected with the preparation-room is a small dark room for the storage of chemicals. These rooms serve also as apparatus and store rooms for the laboratories on this floors.

Leaving the lecture-room from the opposite corner from which we entered, and passing through the laboratory and study of the professor of chemistry [*Prof. Nicholson's*], we come to the balance-room and library. This room is very well supplied with books of reference and the current periodicals, having complete sets of the *Berichte, Fresenius Zeitschrift, Chemical News, American Chemical Journal, Centralblatt*, and others. No special room has been set apart for collections. It is the intention to utilize the corridors for this purpose.

The tables (Fig. 5) in each student work-room, except laboratory B, are ten feet long, four wide, and three feet and three inches high. Four students use one table; each having at his disposal, for storing his apparatus, two large drawers and two roomy cupboards, all secured by a single lock. Each student has two gas connections and an abundant supply of water.

FIG. 5

Chemical Laboratory Student Bench, 1887

The arrangement for water-supply is different from that usually employed. Instead of two basins placed at the ends, one larger oval basin, twenty-one by sixteen in inches, is sunk in the centre of the table, its long diameter across the table, and is supplied from two taps, one at each side. This arrangement has the advantages of being economical, convenient, and neat.

The work-places are numbered consecutively in each laboratory, and are supplied with sets of reagent bottles, bearing, in enameled letters, the name of the re-agent and the number of the desk. The stopper of the bottle bears a number corresponding to the one on its body. By this means a bottle out of place can be easily relocated, and the transposition of stoppers is inexcusable.

In laboratory B, tables are similarly equipped, and constructed on same general plan, except that they are twenty-six feet long and accommodate ten students each. Besides table-supply, each laboratory has a large sink for use when large quantities of water are necessary. Distilled water is furnished on each floor. The building is heated throughout by steam from a central station in the main building. Fire-protection is afforded by sections of hose on each floor, connected with a standpipe which passes up through the centre of the building from basement to attic.

We have now been in occupancy about one year, and feel well satisfied with our arrangements, though some matters of detail await the necessary funds to carry them into effect.

H. H. Nicholson

Bay City Tribune, Special Edition (Michigan)
November 1887

SALT OF THE EARTH.
Michigan, the Greatest Producer of the Saline Article
in the United States.
And Bay City the Second Largest Producing Point in
the State of Michigan.
Ten Thousand Barrels in 1860; Five Million Barrels in
1887—An Astounding Growth.
The First Well---First Companies---Their Output---
Scale of Prices---Present Situation.

To the late Dr. Douglass Houghton, a former state geologist, belongs the credit of establishing the belief in the minds of the people that a great portion of the Saginaw Valley rested upon a bed of salt. [*background history omitted*]

Bay City was not slow to engage in the business. As early as March, 1860, two companies were organized. [*details omitted*].

By the close of 1864, there were twenty-six salt manufacturing firms in Bay county. The manufacturers, capital invested and product were as follows:

KAWKAWLIN.	Invest.	Brls.
O. A. Ballou & Co.	$40,000	3,000
F. A. Kaiser	20,000	6,000

BANGOR.	Invest.	Brls.
F. Lloyd	20,000	1,800
Beckwith, Moore & Smith	16,000	700
Leng, Bradfield & Co	20,000	4,000
Taylor & Moulthrop	10,000	600
Moore, Smith & Co	5,000	

[*Also entries for Salzburg, Bay City, and Portsmouth*]

Total	$622,000	167,328

The Hesperian (University of Nebraska Student Newspaper); October 5, 1887, p. 5

HALL HAPPENINGS.
The faculty has been increased by the addition of Mrs. Rachel Lloyd, Ph. D., University of Zurich, as Associate Professor in chemistry. The lady has been a special student at Harvard and in London at the Royal School of Mines and had taught in Philadelphia and in the College of Pharmacy at Louisville.

Omaha Daily Bee
June 13, 1888, p. 1

Trouble at the Varsity.
LINCOLN, Neb., June 12 — [Special Telegram to THE BEE.] — Four regents met in almost secret conclave to-night—Mallalieu, Hull, Roberts and Gere. There was merry music promised, but it will not take place until to-morrow. In the reading of the minutes a discussion arose on a motion made by Roberts to have the matter of Mrs. Lloyd's appointment as chemist referred back to the faculty on account of being irregular, as charged by the chancellor. Mrs. Lloyd, according to the chancellor, is an infidel. The chancellor claimed that the chairman failed to put the question. Mr. Roberts claimed he did. A lively time is expected to-morrow,

Gere, the chairman, believing that he put the question.

Charles E. Chowins, the superintendent of construction of the industrial hall on the university grounds, claimed that the architects had failed to furnish any plans and that the work on the building so far was wretched; that nothing had been done in a businesslike manner; the walls were already cracking; and as the architect had already received $1,000, he should be made to furnish other plans. The idea of going ahead with a large building, with continual disputes concerning the plans and no specifications, shows the haphazard and general style of doing business by the university committee.

It is expected to-morrow a great fight will take place on the matter of retaining Billings, a scientist, experimenting in hog cholera and other diseases of domestic animals. Half of the board will also attempt to dismiss the chancellor. Charges are to be preferred against him unless matters are settled. Prof. Wing, who has made a farce of the college farm, resigned to-night.

Omaha Daily Bee
June 14, 1888, p. 5

Chancellor Badly Mixed.

LINCOLN, Neb., June 13 — [Special to THE BEE.] — In an interview with Chancellor Manatt of the university, he denied that he had stated that Mrs. Lloyd was an infidel. He did not want it printed. That statement that he had accused the lady, who is a chemist in the university, was corroborated by two regents. It is not a confidential matter that the fight between Billings and Manatt is purely personal. It is predicted that the final result will be the "firing" of both of them.

The resignation of Wing was the result of THE BEE's investigation. It seems that he was afraid that if the truth was told, concerning his past as superintendent, an indignant people would demand his resignation. The college farm, supported by the state at enormous expense, has always been a failure. During the last year but seven students attended and they all bore witness, in a written statement, now in my possession, that Wing was incompetent and the farm a

mistake.

AL. FAIRBROTHER.

University of Nebraska Board of Regents
(University Archives; Papers 1/1/1, box 7, folder 62)
June 15, 1888

[Chancellor Explains Himself to Regents]

He has understood, and continues to suppose, that Mrs. Lloyd is a communicant of the Episcopal ch[urch] — though this is only an inference from the fact that, prominent and influential among the testimonials on which she was appointed here, was one from the Bishop of Kentucky in which (if the Chancellor's recollection is not at fault) she is spoken of as an excellent Christian lady.

University Studies (University of Nebraska)
October 1888, Vol. 1, No. 2. pages 1-22

[This is Lloyd's translation of her thesis for publication in the journal initiated by ex-Chancellor Manatt.]

I.—On the Conversion of Some of the Homologues of Benzol-Phenol into Primary and Secondary Amines.

by RACHEL LLOYD.

VARIOUS experiments, attended with but little or no success, have been made by distinguished chemists at different periods of time to convert benzol-phenol into aniline.

Some years since, Professor V. Merz and W. Weith obtained aniline, together with diphenylamine, by heating benzol-phenol and zinc-ammonium-chloride at a temperature of 280-300°. Later experiments, made in the laboratory of Professor Merz have shown that the above-mentioned changes take place more readily when ammonium-chloride is added to the zinc-ammonium-chloride and the temperature is raised to 330°. Under these conditions, the three cresols have been converted into the corresponding mono- and di-tolylamines, as well as the xylenes into primary and secondary amines. It has been further proved that zinc-ammonium-bromide and ammonium-bromide produce similar results to those given by zinc-ammonium-chloride and ammonium-chloride.

In order to ascertain whether the above

reactions are common to the benzol-series, or not, I have undertaken the conversion of some of the higher homologues of benzol-phenol into primary and secondary amines, with the following results.

[The *remainder of the paper is omitted.*]

Hayden [later Haydon] Art Club Minutes (UNL Archives) 1888-1893

Hayden Art Club Minutes, 1888-1893

Lloyd, Rachel Mrs. is listed as a member in 1888, 1889, 1890, 1891, 1892, and 1893.

October 12, 1888: A request was made that Dr. Lloyd and Mr. Howard prepare papers for a future meeting.

April 1889: Mrs. Lloyd present
November 12, 1889: Mrs. Lloyd present
December 1889: Mrs. Lloyd present
November 24, 1890: Mrs. Rachel Lloyd of the Board of Directors also tendered resignation which was accepted.

The Daily Picayune (New Orleans, Louisiana) Sunday, December 2, 1888, p. 6, c. 3

[Dr. Rachel Lloyd Lectures on Ceramics]

Dr. Rachel Lloyd, associate professor of chemistry at the Nebraska State University, talked on "Ceramics" at the last meeting of the Lincoln, Neb., "Hayden Art Club."

Annual Report Nebraska State Board of Agriculture for the Year 1888, Prepared by Robt. W. Furnas, Secretary Nebraska State Board of Agriculture, Lincoln, Neb., State Journal Company, Printer, 1889, page 80

The Sugar Beet Industry

Read before the State Board of Agriculture at its annual meeting by PROFESSOR RACHEL LLOYD, State University.

An industry which has increased in its annual production, in the space of time bounded by the years 1811 and 1880 from 13,000,000 pounds of beet root sugar to 1,500,000,000 pounds, seems to fix our attention and demand our closest investigation.

In tracing the history of this industry, we find that about the year 1747, Marggraf, a celebrated chemist in Berlin, discovered crystals of sugar in the red beet. He also found that, treated with alcohol, the white beet yielded $6\frac{1}{2}$ per cent, and the red variety 4.6 per cent of sugar. Although the accounts of the discovery came during the Continental war, when native products were in demand on account of the difficulty and expense of obtaining foreign articles. Wagner tells us that the first Napoleon supported the new product in the pursuance of his continental system of excluding cane sugar from the French market, and a trial of the German method was made; but it was not crowned with success until ten years after the downfall of Napoleon the First.

In Germany the efforts of growers of sugar beets have been directed in the development of beets giving a juice rich in sugar, as the excise duty on inland sugar is calculated on the roots. Previous to the year 1881, an entirely different system prevailed in France. In that country the inland duty was calculated on raw sugar; hence the French cultivator bent all his energies toward the production of roots of an immense size, yielding great weight per acre. Since 1884 the French manufacturers have had the power to choose whether the duty should be levied on the roots or on the raw sugar. Whether or not, there are wiser and better ways to protect our industries and increase the revenue in the United States than by a tax on sugar, is a question worthy the wisdom of our legislators.

Of the two varieties of beets — the white and the red — the white is preferred on account of its purity of color and greater yield of sugar. In Germany, the Silesian, Imperial, White French Imperial, and Vilmorin seeds are generally used. The success of the beet sugar industry in Europe has been due in a great measure to a judicious selection and consequent improvement in the seed, the ordinary forage beet yielding only five or six per cent of sugar, while the improved varieties give as high as twenty per cent of sugar.

Climate and soil also exert a marked influence on the percentage of sugar. In considering the influence of these two factors — climate and soil — the commissioner of agriculture at Washington suggests the study of the following points:

1. The kind of climatic conditions. 2. Kind of soil. 3. Kind of fertilizers. 4. Varieties of beet. 5. Effect on soil.

He further recommends that arrangements be made with the agricultural college of each state, or other reliable institutions, to carry on experiments in the directions indicated.

[*Several paragraphs omitted, most of which discussed the rainfall and soil in other states.*]

In the fourth annual report of the board of agriculture, Prof. S. R. Thompson has given results of the sugar beets raised on the college farm during the summer of 1872. Other attempts have been made to cultivate the root in various parts of the state; of the success or failure of these efforts I have been unable to obtain definite accounts. By the courtesy of Mr. Arthur B. Perkins and Mr. H. T. Jul. Fuehrman, I am able to give you some particulars of the beet culture at Grand Island during the summer of 1888.

The seed planted at this place was obtained from the agriculture department at Washington, D. C., and consisted of ten varieties of seed. The seeds were distributed among the farmers some of whom reaped an abundant harvest, and some the reverse.

Messrs. Perkins and Lubbe were the recipients of the best seed. The seed planted by Mr. Perkins was the French White Imperial and was sown in a light sandy soil. Mr. Lubbe planted Vilmorin seed in heavier soil. The yield on Mr. Perkins's farm was from fifteen to twenty tons per acre, despite the fact that the seed was sown six weeks too late; and the plants were without cultivation. Mr. Fuehrman sums up the average results of sixty plantings in the following soil, twelve to fifteen tons. Cultivation will probably increase this average to fifteen to eighteen tons in the former case, and to eighteen to twenty-one in the latter.

Chemical analysis of these beets have been made at Washington, in various laboratories in Germany, by Prof. Huch at Grand Island, and by myself in the chemical laboratory of the State University. I read Prof. Coleman's letter and report of analyses, also analyses made abroad.

WASHINGTON, NOV. 3, 1888.

DEAR SIR:—The sample of sugar beets sent here by you for examination have been analyzed in the chemical division with the following result: Sample 6077 grown by Lubbe (Vilmorin.) Sample 6078 grown by Perkins. (White Imperial.)

	6077.	6078.
Total solids in the juice	18.40	18.80 per cent
Sugar in the juice	15.38	15.76 per cent
Purity coefficient of the juice	83.50	83.77 per cent

The above analyses show that these beets were of a very rich quality, and capable of producing not less than 230 pounds of sugar per ton. If beets of this quality can be grown in large quantities in your locality, it certainly would indicate you have fine soil and climate for the production of beet sugar. Respectfully,

NORMAN J. COLEMAN, *Commissioner of Agriculture.*

Dr. Fruehling, of Braunschwieg, Germany, reports as follows: Sugar 14.4 per cent. The roots examined were slightly damaged in transportation. The analyses made by Dr. Hugo Schultz, at Magdeburg, Germany, confirms the above: Two beets from Perkins, 14.4 per cent sugar; two beets from Lubbe, 15.5 per cent sugar. The third analysis was made by Dr. Muller, director of the beet sugar factory at Ottleben, Hanover, Germany. He reports sugar 13.0 and 15.8 per cent. Another analysis was conducted by Dr. Lanke, director of the sugar factory at Treudelbusch, Germany, with the following results: Sugar 15.2 and 15.9 per cent. The beets sent to Germany were damaged by the long journey, and by the opening and closing of air-tight boxes in which they were sent, hence the percentages of sugar fall below those of the beets analyzed in America.

The average of twenty-six analyses made by Prof. Huch at Grand Island is 13.9 per cent of sugar, the lowest percentage obtained being 9.4 per cent, and the highest 19.2. Of the six analyses made in the chemical laboratory of the University, the average per cent of sugar was 15.8, and the highest per cent obtained was 17.5 and the lowest 13.6. The beets I analyzed were grown by Mr. Perkins, from French White Imperial seed. Out of sixty plantings at Grand Island, no "woody beets" were found.

Should future experiments confirm the work

already done, we have reason to prophesy a great future for the beet-sugar industry of this part of the state at least.

From a financial point of view, the sugar-beet crop must be a profitable one to farmers. Taking fifteen tons as an average yield per acre, and $2.50 as the average cost of production per ton, and $6 as the average price paid at the manufactory for raw beets, we get a profit of $52.50 per acre for the producer.

Or, supposing the yield as shown in table:

YIELD IN TONS PER ACRE	Cost per ton of raising	Price per ton at factory	Income to producer per acre
10	$3.00	$5.00	$20.00
12	3.00	6.00	36.00
15	3.00	8.00	75.00
30	3.00	8.00	150.00

But this is not all — there is a still further benefit. I refer to the effect of the beet crop on the soil. Permit me here to quote from one wiser than I in agricultural lore: "Properly carried on, the cultivation of the sugar beet is greatly beneficial to other agriculture. The deep and careful cultivation which the beet requires greatly improves the land, the soil becoming thereby deepened, and the disintegration and solution of the mineral constituents greatly accelerated. The tap-root of the beet descends to a great depth, loosening the subsoil and drawing the greater part of its nourishment from a depth of soil which most other plants fail to reach. The nourishment thus obtained passes partly into the leaves, and is left with them upon the ground after the gathering in of the crop. When the sugar manufacture is carried on in connection with the beet culture, all of the constituents of the beet, with the exception of the carbon obtained from the atmosphere, can be returned to the land, since the refuse of the factory — the heads of the beets, pressings, molasses, etc. — is consumed by farm stock and becomes converted into fertilizers, while the residuary products and the bone black used are either immediately, or after preparation, incorporated with the soil."

Granted all these conditions, is it too much to think and hope that your honorable board may consider the question of the best ways and means by which experiments in sugar-beet culture may be carried on in a truly scientific way all over the state, thus enabling the state to reap the advantage of an industry which gives such encouraging promise at Grand Island.

Mosaic (Ogontz School Student Magazine) October 1889

[Former Teacher Is Now a Professor]

One of our former teachers, Mrs. Rachel Lloyd, Ph.D., now professor of analytical chemistry in the University of Nebraska, was elected a Fellow of the American Association for the Advancement of Science at its last meeting held in Toronto.

The Hesperian (University of Nebraska Student Newspaper); December 16, 1889, vol. 19, no. 6, p. 3

THE UNIVERSITY AND BEET SUGAR.

Nearly every Nebraskan has heard more or less of the attempt to make the production of beet sugar a Nebraska industry, but few are aware of the prominent part taken in the investigations by the University. The interest of the chemical department in the matter began some years ago when Professor Nicholson was in Germany. He noted the similarity of soil between that of Northern Germany, given up to beet culture, and that of western Nebraska. He thought that beet culture might be made profitable in this state. Some experiments had been made by Germans at Grand Island. Within a year the Wellfleet company of English capitalists have started works in Lincoln county. Now capital wants to know how much sugar the Nebraska beet will yield, and where beets can be profitably raised. These questions the chemical department of the University has undertaken to answer. The department of agriculture distributed seeds to all who would plant and report results. Last spring the University sent circulars to the farmers of the state requesting that sample beets be sent for analysis. During the summer Professor Nicholson and Mr. Herbert Marsland made a trip to the western part of the state collecting soils for analysis. Much literature on the subject of beet-sugar was also collected.

Beets began to arrive at the University in July

and are still coming from all parts of the state. Thirty counties are already represented. Mr. Herbert Marsland in connection with Professor Rachel Lloyd has had charge of the analysis, which began in August. First, beets grown on the college farm were analyzed repeatedly, at intervals of a week, to determine the time when the beets contained the most sugar. Mr. Marsland made a small quantity of beet-sugar which was exhibited at the state fair and since then at St. Louis, New York, and Philadelphia. Both Mr. Marsland and Professor Lloyd have worked faithfully for the last four months and have each now analyzed about eighty specimens.

The process of determining the per cent of sugar may be interesting to the uninitiated. The beets are first washed, then weighed. Then the rough exterior is scraped off and the beet is weighed again. A wedge-shaped piece is cut out of the center, containing proportionately the same amount of exterior and interior as the beet itself. 200 grammes of this wedge are taken and grated to a pulp, which is pressed until it yields up all its juice. After the specific gravity of the expressed juice is determined, 50 c. c. are treated with sub-acetate of lead which purifies it by coagulating the protoplasmic matter. The solution, doubled in volume by the addition of water, is then carefully filtered and placed in a tube of the polariscope. The per cent of sucrose, or real sugar, is shown by the refraction of a ray of light. The per cent of glucose is estimated by treating with a solution of copper (Fehling's solution.)

The results so far obtained are encouraging. The per cent of sugar varies from 4 to 22. It is profitable in Germany to produce sugar from beets containing only 9 per cent. The seed sent out was poor, and the varieties were badly mixed. The beets send in were frequently the largest obtainable and these show a smaller per cent of sugar than smaller beets. Then, too, the plant is not yet acclimated. Under more favorable conditions better results may be looked for. The analyses have not yet been tabulated so as to show the most favorable localities, but indications point to the region extending southwest from Grand Island, embracing the sandy land adjacent to the Platte, as the future home of the sugar-beet.

The result of the investigations will be published in a bulletin early in 1890, and will thus reach all persons interested. We might remark in passing that all this investigation is made by the University without any extra expense of appropriation.

Mr. Marsland's connection with the beets does not end with the operation detailed above. He has undertaken for his thesis-work the determination of the relation between the other mineral matter in the beet and the sugar, and their dependence on the quality of the soil. The beets are weighed first fresh, then dried and then burnt to the ash; and the relation between the different weights determined. The ash is then analyzed both qualitatively and quantitatively, and taken in connection with the nature of the soil the beet grew in, the results from the different beets are compared. So far as the chemical department has been able to discover, this analysis has been undertaken for the first time in this country by Mr. Marsland. The soil anslysis which furnishes part of the basis for Mr. Marsland's conclusions is performed by Mr. Fulmer and Mr. Duncanson, and furnishes further material for thesis work.

Capital City Courier (Lincoln, Nebraska)
Saturday, January 11, 1890

[Browning club organized]

A Browning memorial meeting was held Wednesday evening at the home of Mr. and Mrs. A. J. Sawyer. The program was provided by Prof. Menzendorf, Miss Cochran, Mrs. Jones, Mrs. T. H. Leavitt, G. W. Gerwig, Prof. Rachel Lloyd, H. J. W. Seamark, Miss Elliott, Prof. Sherman and Rev. Chapin. A Browning society was organized with the following officers: President — Dr. A. Marine; vice presidents — Mrs. S. C. Elliott, Mrs. C. H. Gere, Mrs. R. H. Oakley; secretary — Mrs. M. D. Welch; corresponding secretary—Prof. L. A. Sherman; treasurer — H. H. Nicholson; executive committee — Mrs. L. C. Richards, Mrs. J. L. Underwood, Mrs. C. T. Brown, Rev. E. S. Ralston, Prof. L. E. Hicks; committee on work and entertainments — Mrs. George Wing, Mrs. D. L. Brace, Miss Phoebe Elliot, Mrs. A. S.

Raymond, Rev. E. H. Chapin.

[*Robert Browning died December 12, 1889; he was the most celebrated Victorian poet; Andrew Sawyer was the mayor of Lincoln 1887-1889; Menzendorf and Cochran were musical professors at the University who would soon marry; Rev. Marine was a Methodist Episcopal minister; Lucius A. Sherman was Professor of English; Will O. Jones was on the Executive Board of the Nebraska State Historical Society (NSHS); Rev. Dr. John Amsden Chapin was a Methodist minister; Charles H. Gere was publisher of the newspaper and President of the Board of Regents; G. Wing was Prof. Sherman's student; DeWitt Brace was Professor of Physics; Leslie E. Hicks was Professor Geology; Phoebe Elliott was a prominent grade school teacher, after whom Elliott Elementary School is named.*]

Capital City Courier (Lincoln, Nebraska)
March 1, 1890

[Browning Club meeting]

At the meeting of the Browning club on Wednesday evening Rev. Dr. Marine discussed Browning's spirituality, Mrs. Will O. Jones rendered a piano number, Mr. and Mrs. W. J. Lamb expounded the poem "One word more," Miss Jennie Marine sang "My Star," Miss Marion Kingsley read a paper on "Some personal characteristics of Browning" and S. L. Geisthardt expounded "Larshish, the Arab physician." Mrs. Lloyd, Mrs. Leavitt and Rev. Dr. Chapin were made a committee to complete the constitution.

[*Rev. Dr. Abijah Marine was married to Mary Miller and their daughter was Jennie (1862-1944); Jennie's mother died when she was 3; Jennie was a school teacher in 1888 and married Cyrus E. Sanderson in 1891; Mr. W. J. Lamb was an early Lincoln lawyer and founding member of the Lancaster County Bar Association in 1872; Stephen L. Geisthardt (1863-1924) worked in the Bankers Life Building and was NSHS Treasurer.*]

Association for the Advancement of Women
18th Congress of Women in October 1890, Toronto, Canada, Proceedings published 1891

18th Congress of Women, October 1890
Standing Committee: Science (p. 6)
Prof. Rachel Lloyd

Members by State: Nebraska (p. 11)
Brace, Mrs. Eleanor K., Lincoln
Colby, Mrs. Clara Bewick, Beatrice
Leavitt, Mrs. Lura E., Lincoln
Moore, Miss Sarah Wool, 1730 D St., Lincoln
Ripley, Miss Mary A., Kearney
Simpson, Mrs. Julia K., Wolverine Ranch, N. Platte
Weeks, Mrs. Sarah C., 1327 H St., Lincoln
Wing, Mrs. Mary E., Lincoln

Committee on Science (p. 34)
by Mrs. Henriette L. T. Wolcott, Chairman

In the University of Nebraska, in the department of Chemistry, Dr. Rachel Lloyd, a member of the A. A. W., reports a valuable paper on the manufacture and testing of sugar—beet sugar. She has the only position on the staff of an experiment station and the Bulletin is XIII. Mrs. Ellen H. Richards in connection with Dr. Drown has given to the Massachusetts Board of Health a most valuable report on the potable waters of the State and Miss Bragg, formerly of the Institute of Technology, now of Wellesley College, a paper on the Comparative Value of Cereals as Articles of Food. In the department of Chemistry at Barnard College, Miss Mary E. Lovering, in charge, reports ten students in attendance. Miss Rosa Bouton from University of Nebraska has made a chemical analysis of the drinking waters of Beatrice, Neb.

The Hesperian (University of Nebraska Student Newspaper); October 15, 1890

ALUMNI AND FORMER STUDENTS.
[p. 5] H. B. Duncanson and Hugo Nelson are chemists in the sugar factory at Grand Island.

STRAY PICK-UPS.
[p. 7] The Grand Island sugar factory sent

down samples of its first product—the first sugar made in Nebraska—to the chemical department.

[p. 8] The U. of N. is taking great interest in the beet-sugar industry of Nebraska. About fifty samples of beets are received by the chemical department each week for analysis; while Professor Fulmer has analysed during the past year several of the different soils of the state.

The Hesperian (University of Nebraska Student Newspaper); November 1, 1890, p. 8

STRAY PICK-UPS.

October 19 the University chemical department analyzed forty samples of beets which ranged from eight to sixteen per cent of glucose sugar. The best of these beets were raised by [*graduate students*] Miss Rosa Boughton [*Bouton*], and Messrs. H. B. Marsland and E. E. Nicholson [*son of H. H.*].

Association for the Advancement of Women
19th Congress of Women in October 1891, Grand Rapids, Michigan, Proceedings published 1892

19th Congress of Women, October 1891
Standing Committee: Science (p. 10)
Prof. Rachel Lloyd, Neb.

Committee on Science (p. 34)
by Prof. Maria Mitchell, Chairman

Schools of Pharmacy have been established in Buffalo and Boston, where equal facilities are offered to women. The finely equipped school at Ann Arbor, needs only a laboratory or other work room, where the putting up of perscriptions [*sic*] shall be taught. Only with this preparation can a woman enjoy the profession of pharmacist at once after graduating with honors. In many of our States the laws regulating the registration of pharmacists are so severe that the boy of twenty who has served as bottle washer and sweeper in a drug store many be registered after taking the same course that the woman does. Yet she is barred out for lack of useful experience of putting up perscriptions [*sic*]. Several women have graduated from these schools and can find work as chemists. Mrs. R. Lloyd, another member has been elected a professor at Lincoln, Neb., after a course of study in Europe. Until some radical change is made on this line, women are virtually excluded from this pleasant and honorable avenue.

Chemistry and Biology (p. 36)
Professor Rachel Lloyd, a member of this committee, reports herself as still at work on the chemical questions involved in the successful culture of the Sugar Beet in Nebraska.

The Hesperian (University of Nebraska Student Newspaper); October 6, 1891

[p. 9] Among the Professors.

The professors of chemistry were all at work in their several departments during the greater part of the summer.

Professor Lloyd took a short vacation about the middle of the summer and made a trip to the eastern states, returning and resuming the general superintendence of the building.

Professor Nicholson took the last two weeks of the summer months for a trip east. He attended there the national science convention and the meeting of the national chemistry society.

[*Rosa Bouton accompanied him. She had just earned her M.A. in Chemistry at Nebraska. While in Boston for the ACS meeting, she visited the lab of Mrs. Ellen Swallow Richards of the MIT, where she learned about her research in sanitary chemistry. Upon returning home, Bouton developed the sanitary chemistry program at the University of Nebraska.*]

[p. 11] The Improvements.

During the summer a large number of improvements have been going on in the buildings and on the campus. Believing an enumeration of these would be of interest to the average student, the following are given:

[*Omitted descriptions of the Main Building, Nebraska Hall, The Amory, and the Hesperian Office.*]

THE CHEMICAL LABORATORY. — Corrugated iron ceilings have been put on in all the rooms and halls, the walls have been repaired and plastered. The ceiling and interior walls have been painted, as well as the exterior. The hoods in the different laboratories have been remodeled and repaired, and a number of new ones added. Two more rooms have been fixed up with working tables and will accommodate sixty more students. Shelving and cases have been made in the store room.

Capital City Courier (Lincoln, Nebraska) December 9, 1891

[Hayden Art Club Meeting]

The Hayden Art club held its regular monthly meeting Tuesday evening at Palladian Hall. A very interesting program was carried out with Mrs. A. M. Hall as leader of the evening. A series of tableaux under the direction of Miss Sarah Wood Moore, illustrating pictures on English artists was followed by papers by Mrs. H. H. Wilson, Mrs. A. J. Sawyer and others. Mrs. Dr. Rachel Lloyd gave a personal reminiscence on Alma Tedenia [*Alma-Tedema*] which was very entertaining.

The Hesperian (University of Nebraska Student Newspaper); February 15, 1892, p. 10

News.

Our sugar school is coming to the front. The reputation is spreading not only over Nebraska and the adjacent states but over the whole country. The following cheering words came from a California gentleman, who is interested in the beet sugar business: "I cannot speak too highly of the benefits, which are bound to result from such a course. You are taking the right steps in the direction most required to developing the beet sugar industry in Nebraska. You may count on my hearty co-operation in every particular, and I will with pleasure give employment to such men as are needed in our establishments from among the number of your students. What we most need to develop this industry and overcome all unjust prejudices is young men trained agriculturally as well as manufacturingly to the requirements of this new industry.

Letter from Acting Chair Rachel Lloyd to Chancellor Canfield, on March 18, 1892.
Reproduced with permission from Archives and Special Collections, University of Nebraska-Lincoln Libraries.
[Lloyd was acting chair from February to September 1892 while Nicholson was in Germany. During that time, she wrote three letters to the Chancellor.]

Letter 1 from Acting Chair Rachel Lloyd

Lincoln, Neb. March 18th, 1892
CHANCELLOR CANFIELD
Sir:

It has been the aim of the Department of Chemistry in the past, to grow with the University and be able to meet the demands of the people of the State as these demands have arisen. In the absence of the efficient, and energetic, director of the department, his substitute endeavors to have this aim steadily in view.

The large number of students attending the first year's course in the Sugar school, together with the requests already received from the United States Department of Agriculture at Washington, and the Oxnard Beet Sugar Co. at Norfolk and Grand Island for trained chemists, seems to warrant the conclusion that we should continue the school another year on a more extended plan, with <u>facilities</u> for doing more advanced work in this special line of investigation.

To meet the demands made upon us by the farmers of the state, and of many individuals without its borders, it is necessary that we have apparatus for the analyses of fertilizers, cattle foods, and dairy products. Almost daily inquiries are made concerning the nutritive feeding value of sugar beets compared with other root crops; also the feeding value of the pulp and cossettes. The Department of Agriculture of the University expects us, as it has a right to do, to answer these questions from the chemical stand-point; questions which can only be definitely answered by direct experiment. For the analyses of these products, we need an almost entire outfit, as this work has never been undertaken by us in a systematic way. If we are to be able to meet the demands of the people we must take up the line of work during the coming year. In connection with the Geological Survey of the State we ought to be able to push more vigorously the work already commenced upon the water, soils, and minerals of the state. In order to carry out these lines of investigation and provide for an increasing number of students, we must project our plans somewhat into the future: therefore I would respectfully ask that a yearly allowance of not less than $1500 be made the department for the purchase of the necessary apparatus and chemicals for the work specified. I would also request a continuance of the appropriation of $800 for much needed assistance.

Our needs for current literature and books of reference upon the chemistry of sugars, fertilizers, and cattle foods are many and pressing, as our library is almost entirely deficient in these respects. I would respectfully request that $250 be given us for this purpose.

Respectfully submitted,

Rachel Lloyd

Letter from Acting Chair Rachel Lloyd to Chancellor Canfield, on April 4, 1892.
Reproduced with permission from Archives and Special Collections, University of Nebraska-Lincoln Libraries.

Letter 2 from Acting Chair Rachel Lloyd

Chancellor Canfield

Sir:

Prof. Nicholson informs me that through the kindness of Fröhling & Schultz at the Braunschweig Sugar School he can obtain exceptional rates in buying apparatus and chemicals and thus avoid the middle men in New York.

In order to avail ourselves of these superior advantages our orders must be placed at once. I therefore respectfully ask that the present appropriation made by the honorable Board of Regents for the Department at the April meeting, and also the unexpended balance on July 1st of this year's appropriation of the Morrill Fund, be placed at the disposal of Prof. Nicholson.

Very respectfully,

Rachel Lloyd

Letter from Acting Chair Rachel Lloyd to Chancellor Canfield, on June 2, 1892.
Reproduced with permission from Archives and Special Collections, University of Nebraska-Lincoln Libraries.

Letter 3 from Acting Chair Rachel Lloyd

TO CHANCELLOR CANFIELD.

Honored Sir:

The efficiency of the Department of Chemistry during the year has been greatly augmented by the refitting of the Laboratory including the completion of the Assay Laboratory and the Store-room, also by the purchase of much need apparatus. When the changes contemplated are completed (the delay being occasioned by the absence of the efficient Director of the Laboratory), we shall have a finely ventilated building, adding much to our comfort during working hours.

The Department congratulates itself upon the appointment of Mr. Lyon as instructor. His valuable work cannot be too highly appreciated.

As the work of the Department is dual in its nature, the report falls under two heads, i. e.; Instruction and Research. Under the first head, we take pleasure in reporting the faithful attendance of most of our students to all class duties and marked enthusiasm which characterized the work. The 227 students enrolled, were distributed in the following classes:

Latin school	87
Freshman	47
Sophomores	23
Juniors	8
Seniors	5
Specials	7
Post-graduates	3
Assaying	11
Photography	13
Sugar Chemistry	23.

The Sugar School began Jan. 5 with an enrollment of 35. Only 23 students were able to continue the work owing to conflict with other classes. The course in the school consisted [*something is missing from the letter*].

These lectures were finely illustrated by means of the apparatus in the possession of the Physical Laboratory. This course in the physics of light was followed by lectures in the Chemical Department on the use of the saccharimeter, methods of setting prisms to obtain a clear field, adjustment of the compensating wedges, methods for testing the accuracy of instruments.

The laboratory work of the course, consisted in analyses of the various products and by-products of the sugar factory. The samples used were obtained from the Norfolk Sugar Factory, during the last campaign. One of the students did some advanced work in the absorption of sucrose by bone black, and the volume of lead precipitate.

The spring term was devoted to a course of lectures on the culture of the sugar beet. The course embraced the following topics:

1. Origin and history of the beet.
2. External characteristics of a good sugar beet, its roots and foliage.
3. Composition and structure of the root.
4. Relation of the leaves to the root.
5. Food of the plant.
6. Relation of the plant to the atmosphere and to the soil.
7. Conditions governing the growth of the plant, and changes during vegetation.
8. Fertilizers, preparation of the soil, planting, cultivating, thinning, etc.
9. Production and improvement of the seed.

The effort put forward this year is in no way commensurate with the subject, and although we may with just pride congratulate ourselves upon this beginning, every effort must be made to straighten, broaden, and deepen the curriculum next year.

The primary object of the school is to prepare men for work in sugar manufactories. A man to do this work, must be more than a chemist; he must have a thorough knowledge of the mechanical and agricultural work pertaining to the subject. In a word, he must be a "Sugar beet expert." True preparation for this work means a technical course for four years; whilst we would not think of outlining a course, it may be apropos to indicate some of the requirements for such a course. First, a model sugar factory is as necessary to a complete course in sugar work as a laboratory to a chemist or a machine shop to a machinist. Secondly, as the raising of beets is of equal interest to the farmers of the State and to the sugar manufacturers, and as the Sugar beet expert is naturally the most capable to handle this subject properly, it would seem advisable that some provision be made whereby the Agricultural students will be able to take lectures and do practical work in the Laboratory and at the Station farm.

Beside the work of instruction, Mr. Lyon has studied the feeding values of beets, of diffusion chips, and frozen and unfrozen exhausted cossettes, also the fertilizing value of lime residues. Researches commenced by Mrs. Lloyd upon the value of electricity in Chemical analysis, and the comparison of methods for the analysis of honey, were abandoned in February. Irrespective of the work of instruction and of analyses for the Station, there have been made, out of "love to the State", 6 assays, 200 analyses of beets, and 50 analyses of waters, lime stones, and drugs. Mr. Fulmer has continued the Chemical analysis of soils, 20 in number. This work will be spoken of more explicitly in the Experiment Station Report. The excellent and enthusiastic work of Mr. Senter, who has had charge of the class of Photography, led to the formulation of the Camera Club. The Club includes in its membership four Professors of the University, one of the Lincoln High School, a number of students of the University, and several honorary members of national reputation.

In conclusion, Mrs. Lloyd desires to make formal recognition of the valuable assistance rendered her by Miss Rosa Bouton and the Messrs. Senter and Avery, as well as, to express her gratitude for the exceeding kindness shown her by the students of the Department.

The above imperfect report is respectfully submitted for the Director of the Chemical Laboratory, by

Rachel Lloyd

Science, vol. 19, no. 488, p. 324
1892
[This *Science* news article is based on Dr. Lloyd's June 1892 letter to Chancellor Canfield]

NEBRASKA SUGAR SCHOOL.

PROFESSOR LLOYD has just made the first formal report of the sugar school at the State university, Lincoln, Neb., of which the following is a summary: The school opened on Jan. 5 with an enrollment of twenty-five students. These students were mostly members of other classes in the chemical department of the university; the only preparation required for entrance being a clear conception of the principles of elementary chemistry, such as may be obtained in some of the high schools of Nebraska.

The course consisted of two lectures a week, with five hours of laboratory work. The lectures as given by Mr. Lyon embraced the following subjects: 1. Chemistry of the sugars; 2. technology of beet-sugar manufacture; 3. culture of the sugar beet.

The lectures under the first head were designed to give the students an idea of the position of sugars as a class in the series of compounds of carbon, and their relation to others of these compounds, together with a knowledge of the properties and characteristics of each of the sugars.

The cause and effect of fermentation upon sugar solutions were carefully studied. Other important principles relating to the manufacture

of sugar, as the compounds of the sugars with lime, melassigenic action [*creation of molasses*], etc., were taken up in order to prepare the student for the complete understanding of the practical applications of these principles in sugar factories.

A discussion of the methods of the analysis used in the laboratory was given from time to time throughout the course.

Under the second head of lectures, the various processes that the beets, juice, and sugars undergo from the washers to the granulator were studied in detail. Both the French and German forms of machinery were described. As each process was studied, the methods of analysis of its products and by-products was referred to. The study of sugar-house control was in this way presented to the student.

During the latter part of the winter term, Professor DeWitt Brace gave the class four valuable lectures on the theory of light. His lectures including the following subjects: 1. The wave theory of light; 2. polarization of light; 3. rotation of the plane of polarization; 4. application of these principles to the polariscope and to the different forms of saccharimeters.

The lectures were finely illustrated by the means of the apparatus in possession of the physical laboratory. This course in the physics of light was followed by lectures in the chemical department on the use of the saccharimeter, methods of setting prisms to obtain a clear field, adjustment of the compensating wedges, methods for testing the accuracy of instruments.

The laboratory work of the course consisted in analyses of the various products and by-products of the sugar factory during the last campaign. One of the students did some advance work in the absorption of sucrose by bone black and the volume of the lead precipitate.

The spring term was devoted to a course of lectures on the culture of the beet. This course embraced the following topics:
1. Origin and history of the beet.
2. External characteristics of a good sugar beet, its roots and foliage.
3. Composition and structure of the root.
4. Relation of the leaves to the root.
5. Food of the plant.
6. Relation of the plant to the atmosphere and to

the soil.

7. Conditions governing the growth of the plant, and changes during vegetation.
8. Fertilizers, preparation of the soil, planting, cultivating, thinning, etc.
9. Production and improvement of the seed.

These lectures were supplemented by practical work at the station farm, which may be continued throughout the summer at the option of the student. The course closed May 6.

Encouraged by this prosperous beginning of the first sugar school in the United States, it is hoped that in the coming year the work may be greatly extended. Several students who have taken the course outlined are thoroughly prepared to do polariscopic work in sugar factories.

The Hesperian (University of Nebraska Student Newspaper); October 1, 1892, p. 8

[p. 8] The Faculty.

Professor Fulmer was in Montana and western Nebraska.

Professor Lyon visited his home in Pittsburg.

Professor Nicholson returned from Europe in August. He spent nearly half a year in France and Germany studying the beet sugar industry.

Professor Lloyd visited Iowa.

[p. 8] The Students.

Our famous "Kid Nick" and Jesse Beecher found employment during the latter part of the summer in the sugar factory at Medicine Lodge, Kan. We understand that they intend to return to school in about a month.

[p. 11] News.

Professor Nicholson has received an invitation to attend the international congress of chemists to be held in Brussels in 1893. The chief object of this congress is to discuss existing methods of analyses of sugar foods and agricultural products, and to secure greater uniformity of methods.

The department of chemistry has just received a direct importation of twenty-four huge cases of apparatus and supplies for the use of students during the coming year. This saves the university a snug sum in the way of importers' fees. Some of the apparatus was very delicate, and was purchased and tested by Professor Nicholson while on his recent European trip.

It is worthy of notice that six university men are at work this year in the sugar stations of the west. Two are at Medicine Lodge, Kas., two at Schuyler and two at Norfolk. This is the result of the careful work of Professor Nicholson in connection with the sugar industry, and is especially due to the establishment of the sugar school and to the special training in the chemistry of sugar production.

The Hesperian (University of Nebraska Student Newspaper); October 15, 1892, p. 15

News.

The University Camera Club met last Tuesday evening and elected the following officers: president, F. Eager; vice-president, Mr. Young; secretary, Miss Rosa Bouton; executive committee, Prof. Lloyd and T. H. Marsland. The club is reported in a flourishing condition and doing excellent work. Those interested in this department are earnestly solicited to be present at its meeting.

Evening Capital Journal (Salem, Oregon)
April 8, 1893

[Lincoln Savings Bank Board of Directors]

Mrs. Rachel Lloyd, professor of analytical chemistry in the University of Nebraska, has been elected one of the directors of the Lincoln (Neb.) Savings Bank and Safe Deposit company.

Chicago Daily Tribune
April 9, 1893, p. 25
[*Written in advance of the Columbian World's Fair.*]

IS A NOTED CHEMIST.
RACHEL LLOYD, PH. D., AND HER DEVOTION TO SCIENCE
She Was the First American Woman to Acquire from a Foreign University the Degree of Doctor of Philosophy by Virtue of Research in Her Favorite

Study—She Was First to Introduce Experiments in Girls' Schools—Something of Her Early Life.

About a half century ago a wee maid made her entrance into the hearts and home of a family by the name of Holloway, who then resided in Central Ohio. Doubtless this little lady was then a mere "robin red-breast" of a babe; she reminds one today of a dear little brown wren that would snuggle lovingly under the house roof. To her, however, belongs the honor of being one of the most advanced of the splendid army of women who, by merit of labor alone, show the world that the capabilities of women have never been fully revealed nor the status of the sex shown in a moiety of its power and versatility.

Dr. Rachel Lloyd enjoys the proud distinction of being the first American woman to acquire the degree of Doctor of Philosophy by virtue of research in chemistry in a European university, and the second feminine representative of the nations to capture the honor, the first being a Russian.

[*Yulya Lermontova passed her chemistry exams in 1874 at Göttingen (with Friedrich Wöhler on her committee) because they would give her a degree based on two years (1869-1871) work on platinum group separation in Robert Bunsen's lab at Heidelberg and then two years (1871-1873) organic chemistry work in A. W. Hoffman's lab in Berlin. Several obstacles prevented her from continuing research for very long in Russia.*]

DR. LLOYD'S DOMAIN—QUALITATIVE LABORATORY.

How did Dr. Lloyd come to fit herself for such a position? It is the oft repeated story, a noble, ambitious soul seeking to rise superior to the trouble and adversity that come to it as he storms in the tropics, without warning. Brought up under the best influences of Quaker home life Rachel Holloway early developed the traits of a

true student. There was not, however, anything of the pyrotechnic in her intelligence; she was distinguished rather by the thoroughness and stick-to-ativeness that she brought to her work. She was ever thoughtful for and appreciative of the efforts of others, and the gracious, unaffected charm of her has always drawn about her a delightful class of people. It was not strange that

THE GATEWAY TO FAME.

Franklin Lloyd, well known in the scientific world, a grave, scholarly man, should find in the merry, charming maiden his heart's mate. At any rate he wooed and won Rachel Holloway for his wife almost immediately after she left school and took her to his home in Philadelphia. Their married life was beautiful and enriched by extensive European travel and society in which the young wife expanded life a flower.

The girl-wife dearly loved to perch herself, with some bit of sewing, in the deep window of her husband's laboratory, which was a part of their home, and, as she became familiar with the apparatus and watched the experiments with wondering eyes, she little dreamed that the same work would one day be hers in even more extended fields. Widowed when young and with abundant means at her command she chose to travel abroad, where her associations were of the most delightful nature.

But Mrs. Lloyd's nature was of too strong and fine a mold to be spent in individual growth alone and the call to active work came in the loss of her fortune. The news of her loss caused her immediate return to America, and she showed her metal at once by refusing all proffers of assistance and applied herself to securing a position as a teacher, and here she learned her first lesson, that of waiting. As a teacher Mrs. Lloyd was first with the Misses Bonney and Dilleye [*Dillaye*], the founders of the Ogontz School [*known as the Chestnut Street Female Seminary during Lloyd's time*] in Philadelphia. Although she was proficient in the languages, as fate would have it she was appointed to fill a vacancy in the department of chemistry. It was then the day of thraldom to text-books, when experimental work

. CHEMICAL LABORATORY IN THE UNIVERSITY.

in the laboratory was unheard of in a girls' school. As the evident perfunctoriness and uselessness of the study as pursued by her pupils weighed upon her in her classes the fascination of her husband's laboratory, with its abundant apparatus, inspired her with a desire to be able to open up the wonderlands of the science to those young minds. She broached the subject to the principals, begging them to give her the attic to use as a laboratory, and their surprise at the idea of a woman and a lot of girls "monkeying" with acids and elements and compounds, thereby endangering the very roof under which they lived, seems truly comical to the student of today. The plucky little woman gained her point, however.

She entered enthusiastically into preparation for her work, and each long vacation found her at the Harvard Summer School, working diligently under the direction of its best instructors. The result revolutionized methods not only in that school with which Mrs. Lloyd was connected but in all girls' schools. Her first original discovery, published in pamphlet form, was issued from Harvard, and bore the title "Certain Acrylic Acids," since which effort her progress has been steady. After being connected with several well-known schools in this country

she entered the University of Zurich, Switzerland, whence she took her degree as Ph. D. in 1887, her dissertation being on "The Conversion of Some of the Homologues of Benzol Phenol Into Amines."

It was not surprising that so dominant a figure as Dr. Lloyd had become in her chosen work should be sought by the vital young educational blood of the Western Central States, and immediately after a sojourn at the South Kensington School of Science in London she accepted a position as Associate Professor of Chemistry in the University of Nebraska. Two years after entering upon her duties she was appointed a full professorship.

Many and tempting have been the offers made Prof. Lloyd to induce her to give her attention exclusively to individual experimental work, but she feels that her mission is filled in her success as a teacher. When pressed as to the distinctive line of her work she modestly assures one that she is "only a teacher of analytical chemistry." In her is found that rare combination of the magnetic and the electric by which she is enabled to urge onward, to compel by the power of fascination which is hers.

As a woman, outside of her work as an educator, the value of her influence over her pupils is inestimable. No young person is long under her teaching without taking on a greater refinement, a loftier ideal, and a new resolution to make the most of the given ability.

Prof. Lloyd has distinguished herself in connection with one of Nebraska's chief and most interesting products and industries, one that bids fair to rival the great sugar industry of the far Southern States—that of sugar beet culture. By the carefully compiled and complete reports, founded on most minute observation of culture and chemical analysis, this industry is no longer one of experiment, but of pronounced and assured success. Her research in this direction has been in connection with Prof. H. H. Nicholson, the head of the sugar beet school in Nebraska. The data thus obtained is issued in bulletin form and has been of the greatest service to beet-growers.

Prof. Lloyd enjoys a membership with the "Berichte der Deutschen Chemischer

Gesellschaft." She is, besides, a fellow of the American Association for the Advancement of Science, and also a member of the Association for the Advancement of Women.

The Daily Inter Ocean (Chicago)
Sunday, May 7, 1893, p. 11, c. 3
[*This paper reported on the Columbian World's Fair.*]

MANY FAMOUS DAMES

A week from tomorrow the first of the great World's Fair congresses will be opened. Following the chivalrous French adage, place aux dames, the initiation of the Columbian conventions will be the congress of women.

The gathering will be notable both in the subjects to be discussed and in those participating in the discussions. Every department of life affecting women—domestic, social, political, and religious, will be considered. Prominent ladies, representative of every nation, will contribute papers and take part in the discussions. Two sessions will be held every day, morning and evening. Commencing Monday, May 15, the congress will continue through the week, closing Saturday, May 20. The following will be the programme of the opening and succeeding days:

[*most of program omitted*]

Tuesday, May 16, Hall of Washington
7:45 O'clock

"Woman in Science," Dr. Mary Putnam Jacobi, New York

Discussion—Professor Rachel Lloyd, Univer-sity of Nebraska; Dr. Mary A. D. Jone; Louise Reed Stowell, Washington, D.C.; Mrs. Leander Stone.

Saturday Morning Courier (Lincoln, Nebraska)
August 1, 1893

The Daily Inter Ocean (Chicago)
Saturday, September 9, 1893, p. 13, c. 2
[*This paper reported on the Columbian World's Fair.*]

A NEBRASKA WOMAN PROFESSOR.

Dr. Rachel Lloyd enjoys the distinction of being the first American woman to receive the degree of Doctor of Philosophy from a European university. Soon after leaving school she married Dr. Franklin Lloyd, well-known in the scientific world. It was in her husband's laboratory that she first acquired her taste for chemistry, but if it had not been for the death of her husband and the loss of her fortune the world would never have known of the capabilities of this remarkable woman.

At the time she first taught chemistry in the Ogontz school [*known as the Chestnut Street Female Seminary during Lloyd's time*] in Philadelphia, instruction in this science was wholly from text-books. Mrs. Lloyd obtained permission to set up the attic as a laboratory, and a new era in the method of teaching sciences in girls' schools was inaugurated.

She spent her vacations at the Harvard Summer school, perfecting herself in her chosen line. After Mrs. Lloyd had been connected with several well-known schools in this country, she entered the University of Zurich. She took her degree of Ph. D. in 1867 [*1877*]. After a short stay at the South Kensington School of Science in London, she accepted a position as associate professor of chemistry in the University of Nebraska and, two years after, she was appointed to a full professorship. In spite of the fact that —she has made original discoveries in the science

72

and has many tempting offers to devote her time to individual experimental work, she feels that her mission lies in the direction of teaching. Dr. Lloyd, in connection with Professor H. H. Nicholson, who is at the head of the sugar beet school of Nebraska, has done valuable work in the line of sugar beet culture. Her first original discovery was published in pamphlet form and is entitled "Certain Acrylic Acids." Professor Lloyd is a member of the "Berichter der Deutschen Chemischer Gesellschaft," is a fellow of the American Association for the Advancement of Science and a member of the Association for the Advancement of Women.—*Religio Philosophical Journal.*

The Hesperian (University of Nebraska Student Newspaper), September 27, 1893

[p. 6] THE FACULTY ABROAD.
Dr. Lloyd has returned greatly improved in health after a pleasant summer on the Atlantic coast, Nova Scotia and Prince Edward's Island.

[p. 13] LOCALS.
Gilbert Lewis has left the University and entered Harvard this year.

G. N. Lewis at University of Nebraska, 1893

In this photo from the University of Nebraska Archives, Gilbert Newton Lewis is in the center of friends on the University of Nebraska campus in spring 1893. Samuel Avery is leaning against the tree.

In 1889, G. N. Lewis, at age 14, was admitted to the University's Latin School, which had been created because there weren't enough high schools. His family had moved from Massachusetts to Lincoln, where his father practiced law. The Latin School's Preparatory Chemistry

course was taught by H. Elton Fulmer (Nebraska BSc 1886, MA 1890). The freshman and sophomore courses (1 General, 2 General, 3 General, and 4 Analytic) were taught by Dr. Lloyd. In fall 1893, the Lewis family returned to Massachusetts, where Gilbert enrolled at Harvard. There, he earned a bachelor's degree in Chemistry in 1896.

The World's Congress of Representative Women
Edited by May Wright Sewall, Chicago and New York: Rand, McNally & Company, 1894, pp. 195-208

WOMEN IN SCIENCE.
Address Written by Dr. Mary Putnam Jacobi of New York; read by Dr. Julia Holmes Smith of Illinois.

[*Dr. Jacobi earned both pharmacy and medical degrees before practicing as a physician in New York City from 1871 to 1906. She published many medical papers as well as fiction. The first three paragraphs of the speech are given below. They make a pitch for women to engage in science. The remainder of the speech describes women who are engaged in science.*]

Those who interest themselves in that modern development of mental activity in women are liable to imagine that this has been aroused equally in all directions. This, however, is far from being the case. The two great activities of modern times are industry and science, and it is precisely in industry and science that women are least conspicuous. In all industrial occupations, it is true, women are largely engaged—they constitute more than two-thirds of all the factory operatives of the world, they throng the workshops, they carry on the retail business of stores—but we rarely find them as yet among the captains of industry, among the leaders, projectors, or controllers of industrial enterprises on any large scale.

Physical science at the present day has opened up a sphere of activity resembling that of industry in an enormous development of details, which can afford useful employment to multitudes of persons of moderate ability, if well trained in technical methods and possessed of patience and conscientiousness. Either original researches [*sic*] of the processes of applied science demand the cooperation of a great number of assistants to perform manipulations involving much labor and time, requiring intelligence and great accuracy, but not necessitating original mental power.

This is a most useful and important field of work for women. Should they enter largely upon it they might still remain as far removed from the position of the scientific thinkers as is that of the factory operatives from that of the mill owner. But the work of a laboratory assistant, though relatively inferior, is absolutely so important, dignified, difficult, and interesting that the women who should or do engage in it may be well satisfied, even when they do not advance to the dignity of original contributors to the science they serve.

[The list of women mentioned includes: Miss Margaretha Palmer, assistant in the Yale Observatory; Miss Chevalier teaches chemistry at the Woman's Medical College in New York; Mrs. Burt G. Wilder assists her husband's anatomy research at Ithaca; Maria Mitchell "was the first American woman to be known in any science" and "was the first female member of the American Academy of Arts and Sciences;" Hypatia; Maria Cunitz; Jeanne Ehime; Marquise du Chatelet; Maria Agnesi; Nicole Reine Lepante; Caroline Herschel; Sophie Germain; Mrs. Mary Somerville; Philippa Fawcett; Mrs. Christine Ladd Franklin; Songa Kowaleski; Mrs. Susanna Gage; Miss Julia Piatt; Marianne North; Miss Eleanor A. Ormerod; Miss Mary Muretfeld; Mrs. Mary Treat; Miss Alice C. Fletcher; Mme. Ragotzin; Dr. Sara Post; Dr. Sara McNutt. In the discussion, Dr. Smith mentioned Emily Nunn, Mrs. Stone noted that women scientists are somewhat hindered by their lack of training in the mechanical arts compared to men, and Dr. Jones "dwelt chiefly upon the adaptation of woman, by both her delicate physical organization and her patience to the minute and long-continued observation necessary to original research" and then discussed two of her medical findings.]

"Woman in Science" by Louisa Parsons Stone Hopkins, in *Art and Handicraft in the Woman's Building of the World's Columbian Exposition, 1893*, Ed. Maud Howe Elliott, ed., Chicago: Rand, McNally & Company, 1894

Woman in Science.

The mind of woman has always shown itself in sympathy with the harmony and beauty of the physical universe. In the pursuit of knowledge she often elects as her favorite paths those which bring her into close relations with nature. Her proverbial propensity to investigate, her acknowledged patience, her delicacy of manipulation, her exactness of detail all find legitimate scope in the nice observation and conscientious work of the laboratory. With advancing education, better equipped than ever before, she responds to the appeal of natural forms and processes. Her eye, and ear, and touch become sensitive, her mental perception keen to note variations of type and modifications of structure.

It is pleasing to record that American women of this generation are entering the various departments of scientific research with enthusiastic devotion.

While college doors were yet closed to the sex, the modern movement for freeing woman from the traditional limitations not having been inaugurated, individual women were often led to study in a more or less isolated way for their own satisfaction. How many herbariums, portfolios of drawings of plant and animal forms, collections of shells, sea-mosses, and minerals have been stored away as private memorials of happy research and experimentation! Field and forest, mountain and shore have been explored for treasures of science, by many a modest daughter of the soil or darling of luxury. A few of these early students, lifted into prominence by the persistency and value of their work, grace the record of woman's intellectual achievement with a fame which we are proud to acknowledge.

Maria Mitchel as a discoverer in astronomical science is a peeress in the realm in that exalted branch of research. [*Further description omitted*]

The name of Miss Eliza A. Youmans is conspicuous as a pioneer in the field of botany. [*Further description omitted.*]

In many high-schools for girls, private seminaries for women, normal schools, or advanced private academies, the natural sciences of geography, geology, astronomy, botany, and zoölogy have been long taught by women with distinguished ability. Now the colleges for women maintain professorships in every branch of science filled honorably and successfully by women. Consult the catalogues of these institutions for their names, flanked by degrees and titles witnessing their learning and their achievements. [*Paragraph and a half omitted about opportunities at colleges and universities.*]

A number of women are catalogued in various parts of the country as curators or museums, as instructors or professors of science in the institutes and colleges, and as deans of faculty. Mrs. Ellen H. Richards of the Massachusetts Institute of Technology, in the department of sanitary chemistry, is widely known. Mrs. Rachel Lloyd of Lincoln, Neb., one of the most noted women in chemistry in this country, took her degree at Zurich. Mrs. Katharine Brandegee of California Academy of Science is curator of a botanical museum. Emily Gregory, Ph. D., of Barnard College, is recognized in botany. Rachel L. Bodley made a catalogue of natural history which was regarded by Prof. Asa Gray as a valuable contribution to science. She filled the chair of chemistry and toxology in the Woman's Medical College of Pennsylvania, and became dean of the faculty. She died in 1888. Mrs. Louisa Reed Stowell, who has been in charge of the botanical laboratory of Michigan University for twelve years, is a member of the Royal Microscopy Society of London, and of many other scientific bodies. She has made over a hundred contributions to current scientific literature, all illustrated by original drawings from her own microscopical preparations. At the Boston Institute of Technology the Margaret Cheney Reading Room keeps in memory the promise of a fair young life happily devoted to the pursuit of chemistry. Grace Anna Lewis of Pennsylvania is well known as an authority on the habits of birds, and has lectured on this subject with great acceptance. Miss Cora Clarke of Jamaica Plain has made an exhaustive collection of galls, fungi, and mosses; Mrs. Lemmon, artist of the California Board of Forestry; Miss Marion Talbot of Chicago University, department of domestic science; and a host of others who fill responsible positions in all departments of science might swell the list far beyond the purpose or limits of this paper. [*Paragraphs omitted about botanists, Mrs. Mary Hemenway the archaeologist, and illustrators.*]

May we not assure ourselves that whatever woman's thought and study shall embrace will thereby receive new inspiration; that she will save science from materialism, and art from a gross realism; that the "eternal womanly shall lead upward and onward?"

LOUISA PARSONS HOPKINS.

The Hesperian (University of Nebraska Student Newspaper), December 1, 1893, p. 10

LOCAL.

Prof. Lloyd spent her vacation in Fremont, as guest of Etta and Vesta Gray. [*Vesta Gray graduated in 1893 and practiced law in Fremont.*]

The Hesperian (University of Nebraska Student Newspaper), December 19, 1893, pp. 14-15

LOCAL.

Prof. Lloyd has recently organized a class in "history of chemistry."

Dr. White, the successor of Prof. Frankforter, arrived on the 2d. The doctor is a graduate of Johns Hopkins University, and comes here very highly recommended.

Prof. Nicholson left for Florida December 14. The professor and his doctors decided that a change of climate was necessary for his recovery.

The Nebraskan (University of Nebraska Student Newspaper), May 23, 1894

LOCAL.

Mrs. Rachel Lloyd left Sunday for Chicago where she will make her home in the future. Dr. Lloyd is one of the few professors who has the gift of always seeming to take a personal interest in each one of the pupils and in consequence there is not a student who has had work in the Chemical department who will not feel a sense of loss at Mrs. Lloyd's departure. In the long time she has been connected with the University Mrs. Lloyd has done a wonderful work in building up the Chemical department, how large a place she has filled will only be realized when she is gone. The love and good wishes of all her pupils go with her to her new home. [*She is not listed in the 1895 or 1896 Chicago City Directories*]

The Hesperian (University of Nebraska Student Newspaper), June 9, 1894, p. 2

[Lloyd Resigns; by editor Willa Cather]

Because of ill health, Dr. Lloyd has decided to resign her position as associate professor of Chemistry in the University. We ought to be used to this time to losing our chosen ones, but we don't seem to be. Dr. Lloyd has been with us now seven years, and it seems impossible that things can go just right without her. Dr. Lloyd's work must be more satisfactory to her than anything we can say of it. She has seen develop, largely by her efforts and under her eye, one of the largest chemical laboratories in the West. She has seen her lecture rooms crowded by enthusiastic students of all courses and departments. She leaves in Lincoln many warm, social friends, but it is by the students that her absence will be most keenly felt. She has always had a strong personal influence over her students, and possessed the power to awaken that within which passeth show. She is one of those instructors who stand not only for a science or a language, but for ideals and all higher culture. We can ill afford to lose one of these, for their name is by no means legion. Wherever Lloyd may go, she takes with her the gratitude of an institution and of a state where she has helped not only to fashion chemists, but to inspire and kindle earnest young men and women to that culture which society most needs.

[p. 11] HOW THE FACULTY WILL KEEP COOL
Dr. Lloyd will go to the Atlantic Coast.

Hillside Home School Brochure, Seventh Year
1894-1895

HILLSIDE HOME SCHOOL,

[page 3] The seventh year in this Home and Farm School is herein represented. It has passed beyond the experimental period, and its methods, location, and advantages are already familiar to a sufficiently large number of patrons to meet the needs of the school. The capacity is limited to about thirty home pupils and as many day pupils. To new inquirers additional will be given upon application.

The school seeks the patronage of such parents only as are in full sympathy with its aims. These aims are simple habits of life, great attention to the physical well-being of the pupil, close contact with nature, independence of conventionalities. It seeks to be devout, but non sectarian and open in its religious spirit, hospitable to all forms of thought, seeking the underlying unities of faith in the diversities of creed and form. In short, character-building is its aim. It seeks to make self-reliant home-makers and citizens.

[pages 4-7 describe the course of study]
[pages 8-13 describe regulations, such as:]
1. All pupils will be required to devote one hour each day to manual training and home or farm work.
7. For laboratory and shop work girls should be provided with long sleeved gingham aprons, and boys with ticking aprons.

[pages 14-15] PLANS FOR NEXT YEAR.

Important additions have been made in the science department of the school for the coming year. The science room has been fitted up for laboratory work in experimental physics and chemistry, and Mrs. Rachel Lloyd, Ph. D. of the University of Zurich, and late professor of chemistry in the University of Nebraska, has been secured to take charge of the scientific instruction in all grades. Mr. John Bille [*Math, Physics, and Manual Training*] leaves the school for another field of work, and Mr. John B. Steinert, of the St. Louis Manual Training School, has been secured to take his place. Miss Helen Jones [*Singing and Piano*] has leave of absence for one year to further pursue her studies. Her place will be taken by Miss Anna Nell Philip.

[page 16]
FACULTY
ELLEN C. LLOYD-JONES, Principal,
History and Literature.

JANE LLOYD-JONES, Principal,
English Language including Grammar,
Composition, and Rhetoric.

F. W. N. HUGENHOLTZ, JR.,

JOSEPH C. ALLEN,
Greek and Latin.

BERTHA ANDERSCH,
French, German, Piano.

JOHN BILLE,
Mathematics, Physics, Manual Training.

ALICE WARREN,
Natural Science.

MRS. LAURA M. BOOTH,
Art.

M. HELEN JONES,
Singing and Assistant in Piano.

FLORENCE HENDERSHOT,
Violin.

ELSIE M. PHILIP,
Physical Culture and Assistant in Primary and
Intermediate Work.

HARRIET BRADLEY,
Primary and Intermediate Grades.

W. F. KEHL,
Dancing.

JAMES LLOYD-JONES,
Farm Superintendent.

The Courier (Lincoln, Nebraska)
August 25, 1894, p. 12

[Mrs. Lloyd at Hillside Home School]

Mrs. Rachel Lloyd, Ph. D., late professor of chemistry in the university, has accepted a position in the Hillside Home school at Hillside, Wis. She will have charge of the scientific instruction in all the grades. Mrs. Lloyd's friends will be pleased to learn that her health is greatly improved.

[The Hillside Home School was founded in 1887 by Jane and Ellen Lloyd-Jones, who were Frank Lloyd Wright's maternal aunts. The school was co-educational and children learned by doing. Frank Lloyd Wright designed the building as his first important commission but replaced it after his aunts retired with a building designed for architecture students. It is located in the city of Spring Green, Wisconsin, near Taliesin and is 30 miles west of Madison.]

Letter from Mary L. Bonney Rimbaud to Amelia S. Quinton on the History of the Chestnut Street Seminary, September 1894
Reproduced Courtesy of the American Baptist Historical Society, Atlanta, Georgia.
[Rachel Lloyd is not mentioned]

History of the Chestnut St. Seminary.

A paper given to Mrs. A. S. Quinton by Mrs. M. L. B. Rambaut, on the History of the Chestnut St. Seminary of Philadelphia, Pa., copied for Mrs. Rambaut by Mrs. E. H. Kilburn.

Sept. 1894

My dear Amelia,

You ask for the facts connected with the commencement of the Chestnut St. Seminary.

In 1850 I invited my friend Harriette A. Dillaye, to unite with me in a School in Philadelphia, Consulting with a lady of experience (Mrs. Stokes) in furnishing a house, she thought it could be one for $2000.

Neither Miss Dillaye nor myself had half of this amount that we could command, therefore if we decided upon the project money must be borrowed. In considering it Miss Dillaye and her brother did not think it wise for her to risk the little she had. But if I would take the whole financial risk, she would unite with me, and her brother, S. D. Dillaye, would loan me the $2000. To give security for the same, my mother must release a life interest on some property we had in Hamilton, N.Y.

After consideration we arranged as follows—

I was to assume all financial responsibility, and pay Miss Dillaye a Salary of $500. per year — $200. to be paid in cash yearly, and $300. yearly go into the School—until we had each paid an equal amount.

I selected a house, rented it—($900. per year) and bargained for the furniture which was being put into the house.

At this juncture, Miss Dillaye's brother, S. D. Dillaye, decided to go to Europe and could not let me have the money, and passed his obligation over to his brother Henry A. The latter raised only $1400 instead of $2000. This obliged me to go all of whom I had made purchases with the promise of payment soon after delivery, and say I could make only partial payments. This was a great mortification to me.

We went on and opened the School. Miss Dillaye came with five or six boarding pupils. I had secured one boarding pupil and all the day pupils. So far as I can remember the incomes from those coming through Miss Dillaye, and from those coming through myself were about equal. But the prestige from the boarding School was greater than from the day School.

The School quite equaled our expectations in the income of the year, that is, the income would perhaps have met the current expenses. But there was the indebtedness not only of the $1400, but of the much larger expense of furnishing than we had calculated, the furnishing being instead of $2000, over $3000. Of course, I was obliged to borrow, —sometimes here, sometimes there, paying as I had promised by borrowing to pay for borrowed money—but always paid interest when done, and diminished principal as I was able.

I can not express to you the <u>weight</u> of 2 years—the consciousness of the debts never left me—the load might move from one point to another, but it was there, always there.

At the beginning of the 3rd year a sufficient number of my old pupils came from South Carolina to lighten the load.

I could see through—make payments so that I felt comparatively easy. It would take time still to pay all debts but the load was lightened.

Such was the success of the 3rd year that we entered into a written Contract. By its terms I was to continue to bear financial responsibilities and pay Miss Dillaye $500. per year ($200. in cash and $300. into the School) until the indebtedness for house and school furnishings was paid. The net income of the first year following was to be mine as compensation for risks I had borne. This brought us to the beginning of the 5th year.

During the first four years the outlay for the school (above current expenses) had amounted to over $4000.—($4258.00) and it was paid at the close of the 4th year.

The net income of the 5th year, as has been stated, was by Contract to be mine as compensation for the financial responsibility I had borne. I remember we though it a good year.

It was at the beginning of the sixth year that Harriette and I entered into a full partnership,

sharing equally the obligations, financial and educational.

In the handling of larger sums since those first years, the <u>experience</u> of them could alone give any idea of the <u>weight</u> that was borne from borrowing and paying until the indebtedness was met.

Miss Dillaye

Miss Dillaye was of great value to the school. She could combine facts — events and occurrences — so as to convince. This gave her great power over pupils in producing conviction and leading to action. The same influence extended to patrons and friends. She saw advantageous conditions, and could seize them, turning even mistakes to benefits. This was of the greatest value to the School. Miss Dillaye's hopefulness and assurance were an inspiration. The glow of earnestness, interest and devotion (when her heart was enlisted) delighted and charmed. One went from her presence with elasticity and earnest purpose to <u>be</u> and to <u>do</u>.

A feature of the School

From the opening of the school Miss Dillaye had a teacher to room with her, one who from the beginning was a friend, or became so. Naturally as things came up, they consulted and planned, and grew into each other. Just as naturally it was a loosening of our oneness. Conscientiously and able as these women were, (and no praise of them in many ways would be exaggeration) it—was inevitable a separation, more or less, of the Principals. The degree of separation would depend upon the purposes, ambition and power of the teacher. Whatever the influence, and whatever the result, the condition existed (with only a few months of interruption) during our 33 years in Philadelphia.

1888

In 1888 the three, Miss Dillaye, Miss Bennett and Miss Eastman, bought out my interest in Ogontz. Afterwards Miss Bennett gave me a Contract to read, in which Miss Bennett and Miss Eastman had bought Miss Dillaye's interest. Hence both Miss Dillaye and myself were out of the Firm. The Management thereafter was to be

Miss Bennett and Miss Eastman.

Why did I advertise the Dissolution? Simply to give all legal supports to the Contract of Dissolution.

Copy

Form of Notice specially designated to Mr. H. S. Maryland as the one to be used.

Ogontz School

The Partnership existing between Mary L. Bonney, Harriette A. Dillaye, Frances E. Bennett and Sylvia J. Eastman is to be dissolved on July 1st 1888 by the retiring of Miss Bonney and Miss Dillaye. The School is to continue after the above date solely under the able & reliable management of Miss Bennett and Miss Eastman.

"The Westonian" by the Westtown Alumni Association and The Westtown Old Scholars' Association
Vol. 3, Westtown, Pa., Sixth Month, 1897, p. 113
[Rachel Lloyd, Clement's sister-in-law, was probably in the audience when he gave this address at a Westtown Reunion.]

"The Fifties," by Clement E. Lloyd

President, Ladies, Gentlemen and Schoolmates:

My mother, who had been a pupil at Westtown, died when I was eight years of age, and at the tender age of nine (the earliest age at which they would receive scholars) I was entered as a pupil. It was before the railroad was built, when we used to stage it all the way from Philadelphia, a long but delightful ride to us young boys through a beautiful country, and being my first visit from home, it had a fascination and charm for me that I cannot describe.

At home I had never been held very strictly to the plain language, and I shall never forget on the second day at school, with what delight one of the larger boys (I will not mention his name) took me on his knee and pinched me and teased me, so as to get me to say 'now you stop that," and then Davis Reece would mark me for using *plural language.*

I attended the school from 1852 to 1858, twelve terms (with the exception of one winter I was kept home) and of course in such a long period I met with a great many scholars whose

after career it would have been impossible for me to have kept in view, but among my immediate classmates who have achieved success and distinction in the world of business or science, I recall Prof. Edward D. Cope, just deceased, Dr. Samuel Whitall, who settled in New York, also deceased; Dr. Horatio C. Wood, who has long been one of the foremost physicians in Philadelphia; Charles Richardson, who is taking a very active interest in the Municipal League of Philadelphia and working to improve the city government, and Horace Lloyd [*Clement's brother*], cashier of the National Bank of Phoenixville, he having been identified with that institution ever since it started over 35 years ago.

Rachel A. Holoway [*Holloway*], a pupil in 1853 is deserving of especial mention, she having made Chemistry her principal study since, in which she achieved success and distinction, and who, as Prof. Rachel Lloyd, Professor of Chemistry, at Lincoln, was largely instrumental in introducing Sugar Beet Culture into that State.

[Ten paragraphs omitted.]

Then the boys and girls were entirely separate at all times even meetings for worship.

We dined at long plain tables without any of the present accessories of table-cloth, napkins, service, and we ate off metal plates and out of porringers with iron spoons. *[Remainder omitted.]*

Rochester Democratic Chronicle
Friday, June 25, 1897

Reunion of Scholars of the Old Foster School.

———

AT CLIFTON SPRINGS

———

Reception Held Tuesday Evening, Banquet Wednesday Evening and a Musicale and Entertainment Last Evening—Ontario.

———

The reunion of former pupils of the Foster School at Clifton Springs, which has been taking place this week, closed last evening with a musicale in the old Foster School chapel, and with an entertainment called the "Reformation of the World," which was given during former school days, and repeated almost impromptu, with but one hasty reminiscent rehearsal at Dr.

Foster's request. The appreciation of the audience for the burlesque was very manifest. The parts were taken by Mrs. John H. Howe, of Rochester; Mrs. Lillie Hoyt Barnard, of Baltimore; Miss Jennie Valentine, of Bennington, Vt.; Miss Martha Thompson, of Phoenixville, Pa.; Mrs. Jennie Betts Hartswick, of Cloarfield, Pa.; Mrs. E. P. Jackson, of Metuchen, N. J.; Miss Alice Hitchman, of Mt. Pleasant, Pa. The following were heard in the musicale: Miss Janet Loomis, of Attica; Miss Carolyn Dennison, of Clyde; Miss Thompson, of Phoenixville, and Mrs. Lillie Gifford Peck of Phelps.

Yesterday afternoon Mrs. Andrew Pierce gave a tea from 3 to 5 o'clock in honor of the visitors. Yesterday morning was occupied by the reading of letters and greetings from those unable to attend. The banquet on Wednesday evening was an enjoyable feature of the reunion. Mrs. J. H. Howe, daughter of the late Dr. George Loomis, former president of the school, was toastmistress. Toasts were responded to by Mrs. Jennie Betts Hartswick, Miss Valentine, Miss Martha Thompson, Mrs. E. P. Jackson, and Mrs. Lichey. The decorations of the table which was set in the form of an "F" were especially attractive, consisting of a profusion of roses presented by Mrs. Henry Foster; pink satin ribbon and smilax [*a climbing shrub*] were also effectively used. The menu was an elaborate one of seven courses. A pleasant informal reception was the opening feature of the reunion. On Wednesday and yesterday morning a half hour's worship was conducted by Dr. Foster. As a tribute to the memory of Dr. Loomis members of the reunion sent a large ivy wreath to be placed upon his tomb in the cemetery in Attica. Mrs. Rachel Lloyd, a former lady principal, has been in attendance. Mrs. Lloyd is well known for her specialties in chemistry and physics, having been one of the first American women to obtain a degree at the University of Zurich, Switzerland.

[Full list of attendees omitted.]

State of New Jersey Report of Death
March 10, 1900

Rachel Lloyd's Death Certificate
1. Full name of deceased…Rachel A. Lloyd
2. Age…about 60
3. Color…White, Occupation…None
4. widow
5. Birthplace…N.J.
6. Last place of residence…Beverly NJ
7. How long resident in this State…Eight Months
8. Place of death…Beverly NJ
9. Father's name…
10. Mother's name…
11. I hereby certify that I attended the deceased during the last illness, and that…she…died on the…Seventh…day of…March…1900; and that the cause of death was…Heart Failure: A Signal of Paralysis.

    A M Taylor, Medical Attendant
Residence, Beverly NJ
Name of Undertaker, J. R. Davis
Residence of Undertaker, Beverly NJ
Place of burial, Phil^a Pa

Philadelphia Record
March 9, 1900
[An identical notice appeared in *Philadelphia Inquirer* on March 10, 1900]

DIED

LLOYD.—At Beverly, N. J., on March 7, 1900, Rachel Lloyd, Ph. D., widow of Franklin Lloyd. Relatives and friends are invited to attend the funeral, on Saturday, at 2:30 o'clock, at St. Peter's Church Third and Pine streets, Philadelphia.

The Nebraskan-Hesperian (University of Nebraska Student Newspaper); March 28, 1900

MRS. RACHEL LLOYD.

Acting Chancellor Bessey spoke to the students of chapel, March 14, of Mrs. Rachel Lloyd, formerly instructor in the university, who died recently at Beverly, N. J. He said:

"It has been my sad duty a number of times to speak of the departure of those who have been in the university. I want to say a little with regard to one who was a professor in this university for seven years, and who retired six years ago; one who left a very strong impress while here, one whose impress is still felt. Dr. Rachel Lloyd died in Beverly, N. J. just one week ago to-day. She was for seven years professor of analytical chemistry in this university, having been elected to the position in May 1887; and she resigned in June 1894, because she was entirely broken down in health.

"Chancellor Canfield in speaking of her resignation said: "This is another case of an instructor whose health was practically broken in the service of the state."

"Mrs. Lloyd was a woman of rare refinement, coming from an old family in which wealth and refinement had been present for generations. She lived in a home surrounded by all the luxury that wealth could give. Her husband, Dr. Lloyd, was a prominent physician in Philadelphia [*This is second time Franklin Lloyd is called a Dr. and the first time a physician but his only degree was in Pharmacy*]. Her children were also with her. But death came and struck down her husband and children, and then came the panic of '73, '74, '75, and left her penniless. The stricken woman found herself at about thirty-five years of age facing poverty and the need of turning to some employment to earn her livelihood. She became a teacher in a school for girls in Louisville, Kentucky [*School for Girls in Philadelphia and later a Pharmacy College for Women in Louisville*]. Here she labored for many years, teaching during the year and spending her vacations in Harvard university in the chemical laboratory. I heard her say she was drawn to chemistry because her husband was a chemist and because he was interested in that line of work.

"She continued to study at Harvard, taking the work one summer at a time, and at last she was able to go abroad. She studied for two years in the University of Zurich, and in the spring of 1887 this old university gave her the degree of doctor of philosophy for the work that she had done. Immediately after receiving the degree she came to us. I shall never forget the occasion when Professor Nicholson called me into his office in the chemical laboratory in the spring of

'87. The regents had made provision for an additional professor of chemistry, and he wished to confer with me in regard to the matter. Said he, 'I am thinking of nominating a woman for this place.' He said it timidly, and I shrugged my shoulders, because there are not many women chemists, and there were fewer then than now. Then he told me all about her, and read letters from eminent men in Harvard and elsewhere, showing that she was a woman not only of high attainments in chemistry, but a woman of rare attainments otherwise. She came to us and remained with us, working as probably no other professor has worked here, and she worked herself to death in our service.

"She spared not herself. She was not only a trained chemist, she was a great teacher, and more than that she was the beloved adviser and counselor of the students. The young women have lost a great deal because you came to the university after Doctor Lloyd left us. There still lingers on this campus like a sweet perfume the memory of her devoted life. It is your good fortune to be here where these memories still influence your lives. You do not know it, but many of you are still influenced by the life of this strong, helpful woman. It is your misfortune that you have not come into direct personal contact with this refined, devoted, wise and willing friend, adviser, and teacher—Rachel Lloyd."

Nebraska Local Section Meeting
Rosa Bouton's Address, March 1900

Dr. Rachel Lloyd

Dr. Rachel Lloyd was appointed Associate Professor of Analytical Chemistry in the University of Nebraska in May 1887. In recognition of her excellent work, the Regents later gave her the title of Professor of Analytical Chemistry. She served the University faithfully for seven years, and then resigned on account of failing health in June, 1894.

She came to Lincoln first some time during the summer of '87, several weeks before the opening of the fall term. She began her work at once in the chemical laboratory in order that everything should be in readiness for the students at the beginning of the school year. This early coming was characteristic of all her work. She was always on time. I used sometimes to think that she would rather be two hours early than two minutes late. During her seven years' stay here I never knew her to be a moment late anywhere.

Dr. Lloyd was neatness personified. In her dress, in the arrangement of her lecture table, in her laboratory, everything was exceptionally neat and orderly. She believed that whatever was worth doing at all was worth doing well. Whatever she undertook, and she undertook many things, she did it in the best way. I think I never knew any one who took more care of the details than she; consequently every one knew that whenever she did a piece of work it would be well done in every particular. And since did so much work it necessarily follows that she was an indefatigable worker. Eight o'clock in the morning usually found her at the laboratory, and she seldom left at night before six, many times returning in the evening to continue her labors.

She loved her work and succeeded in getting her students to do the same. Her personality was very strong, and at the same time very attractive. One recognized her at once as a woman of broad culture and refinement. Dr. Lloyd had the power of making personal friends of her students and of awakening in them an enthusiasm akin to her own for the study she so much enjoyed. Her influence over young people was wonderful. Accordingly, her greatest work was that of a teacher. Many are the alumni and former students of this University who stand ready to hear loving tribute to her memory.

On coming here she had hoped to continue certain original investigations begun in Zurich where she took her doctor's degree shortly before coming to Nebraska. But the work of instruction was so great that she was not able to carry this plan into effect. She did, however, a great deal of analytical work in addition to her teaching. She was joint author with Professor Nicholson of the first three bulletins on the sugar beet, published by the University. I well remember her giving a paper at the beginning of this study before one of the meetings of a Farmers' Institute held in chapel, and of hearing Professor Nicholson tell with a touch of pride in his voice of the surprise depicted on the faces of the farmers, as they saw a woman beginning a paper on the sugar beet, and then how intense interest took the place of surprise as she continued her reading.

Some time during the winter of '92 Prof. Nicholson was given a leave of absence to go to Europe to make a further study of the sugar beet problem. During his absence Dr. Lloyd was at the head of the Department of Chemistry with all that means, The following summer she took charge of the Chemistry in the summer school.

Although most of her time and energy was expended at the University, she found some time for other things. In the Spring of '89 she was elected to a place on the Board of Directors of the Haydon Art Club, which position she held for about a year and a half. She was very much interested in art and was a valuable member of the Board of Directors of that Club.

Socially she was a great favorite and had many warm friends among the people of Lincoln. She was very kind and thoughtful of the welfare of others, even though such kindness might mean the sacrifice of her own comfort.

Dr. Lloyd was a very pleasing speaker. She had a deep, rich voice with good carrying qualities. She spoke distinctly and her choice of words was excellent. She occasionally gave public papers or addresses on subjects not chemical. I recall one of given papers before a Browning Club and another before the Hayden Art Club.

In regard to her own life and affairs, Mrs. Lloyd was very reticent. Few of her friends here knew as much of her life history as Acting Chancellor Bessey gave in his chapel talk a short time since.

During the summer of '92 she went as the guest of Mr. and Mrs. Weeks to the Black Hills. While there she was struck with paralysis from which I think she never recovered fully. She had an unusually strong will and was determined not to give up. During the two years which followed she bravely fought the physical weakness, but finally she was obliged to succumb. She spent the first year after leaving Nebraska in Hillside, Wisconsin, where she taught science in a small private school. Since then she has spent most of her time with friends in Massachusetts, New

York, and near Philadelphia. She died at the home of her friend Mrs. Scattergood in Beverly, New Jersey, her old paralytic trouble having returned with renewed energy.

Dr. Lloyd was a woman of unusual ability. By means of thorough scientific training and hard work she attained for herself a place in the scientific world above that ordinarily reached by a woman. She was one of the first American women to take a Ph. D. in a foreign university. Prof. Mabery, of Harvard, pronounced her the best woman chemist in this country at the time of her appointment in this university. Her name, by the way, appears with Prof. Mabery's on the result of the "Study of Certain Acrylic Acids." She was a member of the German Chem. Gesellschaft as well as the American Chemical Society.

Above and beyond her intellectual attainments she had a kind hand, a loving nature and a large heart. To me the memory of Dr. Lloyd's life is full of valuable lessons. I am thankful that it was my privilege to know her intimately.

Mrs. Lloyd was devoted to her professional and scientific work. She kept an active membership in the various scientific societies, notably The German Chemical Society, The English Chemical Society, The American Chemical Society and the American Association for the Advancement of Science in which she was a fellow. She also was a charter member and an active worker in the Chemical Club of the University of Nebraska; also a member of the Photographic Society of Lincoln. In addition to her more formal lectures she often met her students and gave them an informal talk or popular lecture in order to be sure that the subject matter was perfectly clear to them. Besides this work she gave occasional popular lectures by request before different State societies. She also took an active interest in the development of the sugar beet industry in this State and did an immense amount of valuable work in the furtherance of this business.

Notwithstanding this constant activity in her own especial line of work she found time to interest herself in various other things. Mrs. Lloyd was distinctively artistic in her tastes. She helped organize and was a charter member of the Hayden Art Club and gave much time to its interests in the way of addresses and lectures on art topics. She also had strong literary tastes and was a prominent member of the Browning and Shakespeare Clubs in which she was an active member contributing much to their success in the way of talks, short papers and discussions.

Socially she was a universal favorite and in demand at all University functions. In these various lines of activity she never lost sight of the welfare of her students and managed to give one or two receptions during each year especially designed to advance their interests. To those students and others who were fortunate enough to come into personal relations with her her memory will always be cherished as one who sacrificed herself for the welfare of others.

St. Eeb Ragus Carnival and Street Fair
Fremont, Nebraska
September 10-15, 1900
Reproduced by Permission of Hake's Americana and Collectibles

St. Eeb Ragus Festival Buttons, Sept. 1900

St. Eeb Ragus Carnival and Street Fair button with devil and sugar beet image "Oh Sugar! This Beets me" (2.1 in. diam.). This button sold on Hakes.com for $440 in June 2008

St. Eeb Ragus Carnival and Street Fair button with flower-adorned car "Flower-Parade Souvenir" (1.25 in. diam.).

King Steeb Ragus Carnival and Street Fair button with jester image (1.25 in. diam.). This button sold on Hakes.com for $31 in January 2007.

Rachel Lloyd, Ph. D. (Zurich)
by Clement E. Lloyd, published October 1900

PREFACE.

ALTHOUGH conscious of his inability to do full justice to the memory and character of Prof. Rachel Lloyd, the writer of this brief sketch of her life attempted its preparation for two reasons.

He thought it due to her memory and worth, that recognition should be made of the value to the community of her life work, and that in departing this life, attention should be called to her useful career, high character and lovely disposition, to which so many attest.

Secondly, the poet has said "Lives of great men all remind us, we can make our lives sublime," and I believe that live of great women are just as encouraging, although, as is often the case, the same achievement which in a man is heralded far and wide, if accomplished by a woman, does not get its proper recognition. Prof. Lloyd was a remarkably successful teacher, owing no doubt to her ability to win the love and esteem of her pupils, and by securing their confidence, she was enabled to impart the knowledge she possessed.

Her determination to excel in chemistry and to obtain a degree, in spite of all opposition both at home and abroad (simply because she was a woman), and her success in introducing the culture of the Sugar Beet into the State of Nebraska, redound greatly to her credit as to that of her sex, and entitles her to recognition as a benefactor of her country and race.

Well might we all emulate her entire devotion to the one object of her life, her wonderful will power that enabled her to surmount difficulty, her integrity, punctuality and reliability, and also her business ability which was equal to that of most men, yet with it all retaining those feminine charms of manner and deportment which bespoke the true woman, and made every one who knew her a friend.

Modest and extremely sensitive as she was to all praise and publicity, yet I am sure with her love of doing good, she would not object to these line if they might be the means of stimulating others to duty and helping her young friends to succeed in life.

Though dead, she yet liveth, and her works do follow her for good.

CLEMENT E. LLOYD

Philadelphia,
　　October 1, 1900.

The Westonian by the Westtown Alumni Association and The Westtown Old Scholars' Association Vol. 7, Westtown, Pa., First Month, 1901, p. 2

[Rachel Lloyd Biography Printed]

Clement E. Lloyd, of Philadelphia, has printed for private distribution, a brief memorial of his sister-in-law, Rachel Lloyd, who died at Beverly, N. J., on the 7th of Third Month, 1900. Though a teacher of wide experience, her work was not in connection with any schools of this Society, and she was not, therefore, so well known to readers of THE WESTONIAN as might otherwise have been the case.

She was born at Flushing, Ohio, in 1839, the daughter of Robert S. and Abigail (Taber) Holloway, the latter of a New Bedford, Mass., family. She entered Westtown Boarding School in 1853, and later began teaching in Philadelphia. In 1859 she married Franklin Lloyd. On the death of her husband, in 1865, she resumed teaching, and was prompted to an extensive course of study in preparation for usefulness in her chosen field—that of chemistry. She finally took the degree of Ph. D., at Zurich, Switzerland, being the first Westtown girl, and until quite recently the only one, to attain such distinction. She taught in several different States of the Union, but was most widely known, perhaps, for her connection of several years with the

University of Nebraska, at Lincoln. She was largely instrumental in the introduction of the beet sugar industry in Nebraska, and in many ways left her impress upon the educational and material growth of the country. She was an indomitable worker, and seems to have been much loved and respected by all with whom she came in contact.

The Times (Philadelphia)
January 10, 1901, p. 11

Life of Prof. Rachel Lloyd
An Interesting Biography Prepared of
Famous Woman Chemist.

An interesting memorial biography of the late Professor Rachel Lloyd, Ph. D., of this city, has been completed by Clement E. Lloyd, and is prepared for private distribution among the friends of the deceased scientist. The author was a brother-in-law to Mrs. Lloyd, and his life-long intimacy with her and her work has enabled him to accurately portray her trials and successes in her chosen field.

The book, which is handsomely printed, bearing a beautifully engraved portrait of the late Professor Lloyd on the initial page, contains a complete sketch of her life, and reproduces many of her letters.

Engraving of Rachel Lloyd

Rachel Attie [*Abbie*] Lloyd was born of Quaker parentage in Flushing, Ohio, in 1839, and received her early education there in Westtown, Pa. She was married in this city to Franklin Lloyd, who was then a chemist employed by Powers & Weightman, in 1859. Mrs. Lloyd early began the study of chemistry, and after her husband's death, at Bangor, Michigan, six years

later, devoted her whole life, with the exception of time spent in religious work, to a pursuit of that science. Several years later she became the head of the Women's College of Pharmacy, in Louisville, Ky., but wishing to take a degree, she by began to study of German, and sailed for Zurich, where notwithstanding the opposition of some of the professors, she gained the degree of Ph. D.

Returning to this country, Mrs. Lloyd consecutively occupied the position of principal in a dozen different women's colleges throughout the United States. Her death, which was due to paralysis, on March 7, 1900, in Beverly, N.J., ended a life of great usefulness.

New York Daily Tribune
Wednesday, January 30, 1901, p. 5, c. 2
[Reprinted in the February 9, 1901 issue
of *Woman's Journal*]

Only-Woman's Page
DR. LLOYD'S ACHIEVEMENTS.

A short sketch of the life of Dr. Rachel Lloyd, who died a short time ago, has been published recently. Dr. Lloyd was professor of chemistry at the University of Nebraska, and her degree was conferred by the University of Zurich, where she was a student for two years, which was a great honor, as such a degree in chemistry had been conferred upon a woman only once before by a Continental university.

It was not until she became a widow that Mrs. Lloyd began to study chemistry, although she had become interested in the science because her husband was a chemist. She attended Ratcliffe [*Radcliffe*] for seven years, and then, as there was no college in America where she could obtain a degree, she went to Switzerland.

While in Europe, Dr. Lloyd investigated the culture of the sugar beet, and when she became assistant professor of chemistry at the University of Nebraska, she became convinced that the climate and soil of that State were adapted to sugar beet growing. As the university is at Lincoln, where the experimental station of Nebraska is also located, she, in association with Professor H. H. Nicholson, began experimenting, and in four years the first sugar factory was established. Beet sugar is now a leading industry of Nebraska, and Professor Nicholson says that Dr. Lloyd is entitled to the greater part of the credit as she did most of the work.

Dr. Lloyd was a member of the Deutsche Chemische Gesellschaft, of Frankfort, Germany; the English Chemical Society, the American Chemical Society; a fellow of the American Association for the Advancement of Science, also of the Hayden Art Club, Browning Club and Photographic Society, of Lincoln, Neb.

Proceedings of the American Chemical Society
April 1901, Volume 23, pages 84-85

OBITUARY.
PROFESSOR RACHEL LLOYD, PH.D., ZURICH

Professor Rachel Lloyd was born at Flushing, Ohio, January 26, 1839. She died at Beverly, N. J., May 7, 1900 [*She died March 7*]. She was united in marriage to Mr. Franklin Lloyd, chemist with Messrs. Powers & Weightman, May 11, 1859. After the death of her husband, October 6, 1865, she spent several years abroad for her health. On returning home she was forced, by loss of property, to engage in teaching. In the private school for young ladies of Misses Bonney and Delaye [*Dillaye*], she became interested in science, and in 1876 attended the summer school of instruction in chemistry at Harvard University, which she continued to attend until 1884. As she extended her knowledge of chemistry she was promoted from one position to another, until she determined to devote her energies exclusively to chemistry. On finding that the only obstacle to her promotion to a professorship of chemistry was the fact that she had never received a degree, she resigned a good position in Louisville, Ky., and went to the University of Zurich, Switzerland, then the only place in the world where a woman could receive the doctorate degree. In two years she received the degree of doctor of philosophy with honor, and soon afterward was elected professor of analytical chemistry in the University of Nebraska, which position she held until she was forced to resign on account of failing health.

Dr. Lloyd possessed remarkable energy and force of character, combined with broad culture and great mental ability. To natural refinement and a sympathetic nature she united the culture of the best society and extended foreign travel. These qualifications with a strong and attractive personality, and the power of making personal friends of students, rendered her teaching very effective. In an address to the students of the University of Nebraska after her death, on the value of her service to the University, Acting Chancellor Bessey said: "She was not only an eminent chemist, she was a great teacher, and more than that, she was the beloved advisor and counselor of students."

Professor Lloyd's contributions to science include the following publications, with C. F. Mabery: "On Diiodbromacrylic and Chlorobromacrylic Acids;" "On Dibromiodacrylic and Chlorbromiodacrylic Acids." These papers were published in the *Proceedings of the American Academy of Arts and Sciences*, and in the *American Chemical Journal*.

Inaugural dissertation for the degree of doctor of philosophy: "On the Conversion of Some of the Homologues of Benzol Phenol Into Primary and Secondary Amines." This paper was published in the *Berichte*, **22**, 491, and in *University Studies*, University of Nebraska.

Outside of her eminent work as a teacher, Dr. Lloyd's greatest work at Lincoln was in laying the foundation for the enormous development of the beet-sugar industry in the state of Nebraska. While in Switzerland, she became interested in the cultivation of the sugar-beet, and seeing the great possibilities in its extension in Nebraska, she started and directed the first experimental work. The rapid expansion of this industry was due to the combined efforts of herself and Professor Nicholson.

While it is an incentive to the best endeavor to contemplate the rich fruitage of such a life, there is a feeling of sadness that the great temptation to intense effort should result in the early death of so many eminent workers.

C. F. MABERY

Dokumente der Frauen, vol. 5, p. 161
June 1, 1901

Als Professorin der Chemie

an der Universität zu Nebraska (bei Lincoln) starb vor einiger Zeit Dr. Rachel Lloyd. Sie hatte in Zürich promovirt, als zweite Chemikerin in Europa, nachdem sie erst als Witwe sich dem Studium zugewendet. Dr. Sloyd [*sic*] war Mitglied der "Deutschen chemischen Gesellschaft" in Frankfurt, der English Chemical Society, der American Chemical Society, der American Association for the Advancement of Science, des Hayden Art Club, Browning Club und der Photographic Society in Lincoln, Nebraska.

[*Translation: A female professor of chemistry at the University of Nebraska (at Lincoln) died some time ago, Dr. Rachel Lloyd. She graduated from Zürich, as the second female chemist in Europe only after becoming a widow. Dr. Lloyd was a member of the German Chemical Society in Frankfurt, the English Chemical Society, the American Chemical Society, the American Association for the Advancement of Science, the Hayden Art Club, Browning Club and the Photographic Society in Lincoln, Nebraska.*]

Mosaic (Ogontz School Student Magazine)
1908

[Remembering Mrs. Rachel Lloyd]

[*At a class reunion, Mrs. Cornelia Blakemore Warner, Class of 1877, wrote:*] The sweet, quiet influence of Miss Dillaye's niece, Miss Foote, is not to be forgotten either, and Mrs. Rachel Lloyd, a woman of exceptional social gifts, organized the science-teaching at "1615" in a way truly creditable for that period.

The Pharmaceutical Era 45, p. 103
February 1912

The Louisville School of Pharmacy for Women

The Louisville School of Pharmacy for Women is unique. Inasmuch as it is the sole experiment of the kind that has been made, it is deserving of especial record. This institution was formally organized in 1883, and incorporated March 11, 1884. Its founder was Dr. J. P. Barnum, who died several years ago in the mountains of Kentucky.

The president of the school was Theo. Harris, a banker of Louisville, Ky., and the secretary was Dr. E. A. Grant. Both these gentlemen are dead.

The Louisville School of Pharmacy for Women graduated, as far as can be learned, some fifteen or twenty young women, and then, for lack of patronage, was abandoned by those who established it.

The last annual government report, which was the ninth report of the school, was made for the year 1891-1892. At that time there were 52 students registered. For part of these particulars we are indebted to the kindness of J. W. Fowler, M.D., Ph.D., superintendent of the City Hospital of Louisville, Ky. While this gentleman was never officially connected with the institution, an honorary diploma was conferred upon him in 1892 by the Board of Regents. He says that upon the request of the writer for specific information, he was surprised to find that all those as far as he could learn who had been connected with the college are now dead, nor could he find a single graduate anywhere.

Doubtless some are in existence, but there has been no incentive for the alumnae to keep in touch with each other as a body. From Professor Gordon L. Curry, Dean of the Louisville College of Pharmacy, it was learned that no college building proper was provided and that the instruction was given in the store of J. P. Barnum (now dead) on 4th street between Green and Walnut. Here the practical store work was combined with lecture work, but naturally at something of a disadvantage.

Red Cloud Chief (Red Cloud, Nebraska)
June 22, 1916

Lays Cornerstone for New Building

Prof. Benton Dales, head of the Chemistry department of the state university, laid the cornerstone of the new chemistry building Thursday afternoon. Dean Lyman, of the college of pharmacy, Prof. R. J. Pool, head of the Botany department, and a number of instructors and students were all who witnessed the laying of the cornerstone. Copies of city newspapers, the Daily Nebraskan, the 1916 Cornhusker, university catalog, and a number of photographs were sealed in the box placed within the cornerstone. Included in the photographs were pictures of Chancellor Avery, Prof. H. H. Nicholson, first head of the chemistry department, Prof. Rachel Lloyd, the second head, and photographs of the chemistry societies. A number of chemicals were also placed in the stone.

"Notes on the History of the Ohio Yearly Meeting" 1918-1919 by Watson Dewees, Philadelphia

Excerpts from Chapter 6:
Mount Pleasant Boarding School

School was opened on the twenty-third of First Month, 1837. Daniel Williams, M. D., and wife, Elizabeth, were the first superintendent and matron. Robert S. Holloway and George H. Jenkins were the men teachers, with salaries fixed at four hundred dollars as a maximum. Abby T. Holloway (wife of Robert) and Abigail Planner were the women teachers at two hundred and fifty dollars per year. These four were all residents of Mount Pleasant or the immediate vicinity and are said to have been well qualified. The price of board and tuition was fixed at sixty-eight dollars a year. The total enrollment the first year was one hundred and twenty, but the average attendance was eighty-five. No arrangement for vacations was made at first, but very soon the scholastic year was divided into two terms of twenty-four weeks, and the price changed to seventy-two dollars per year, equal to one and a-half dollars per week for each pupil.

Robert and Abby Holloway, of the first corps of instructors, left in the spring of 1838 on account of the ill health of the former. Parvin Wright and Susanna M. Thomas succeeded them.

[*Paraphrased from Wikipedia: The Mount Pleasant Boarding School was originally called "Friends Boarding School." It was founded in 1837 in Mount Pleasant, Ohio, by the Ohio Quakers who modeled it after the Quaker Boarding Schools in Philadelphia. It became known as the Olney School in the 1840s. In 1854, the regional Quakers split over doctrinal issues. The school became known as the Mount Pleasant Boarding School and operated until 1875. The operation of the Olney School was moved to a new building in Barnesville, Ohio, 15 miles away. The Olney Friends School is still active in 2014 as a college preparatory academy.*]

"Retrospect" by James M. Farron, Abington, Pa. 1960

Chapter 1:
Chestnut Street Female Seminary

A brass plate attached to the front door announced that this building housed the

CHESTNUT ST. FEMALE SEMINARY MISS M. L. BONNEY

The building, located at 1615 Chestnut Street in Philadelphia, was a stately, commodious four-story brick dwelling with green slat shutters, white marble trimming and broad marble steps, and was located in the middle of a row of "fine city residences." The school had been founded at this location in 1850 by Miss Mary L. Bonney and Miss Harriet A. Dillaye, and its history parallels that of women's higher education in this country.

The school Prospectus of 1857 lists the purpose of the school: "While it is the primary design of this Institution to secure to its pupils a thorough and extended education in the varied Departments of Literature and Science, much attention is paid to Music, Painting, Penciling and Crayon. Throughout the entire course a constant effort is made to unit SOLIDITY WITH POLISH."

In the early years there were three classes listed: Junior, Middle, and Senior. A few years later a Graduating Class was added above the Senior Class and in 1879 [*Rachel Lloyd worked here from 1873 to 1880*], about eight 12-year-old girls, relatives of former graduates, were admitted to form a younger class.

An important part of the day's routine was calisthenics, the forerunner of military drill, and walking. The calisthenic uniform of the day consisted of black flannel bloomers, blouse and short skirt, and a red flannel sash with tassel tied on the side.

A good idea of the course content of the school can be gained by considering a list of some of the textbooks from the 1857 Prospectus:

Mrs. Willard's Temple of Time
English and Ancient Chronographers

Burritt's Geography of the Heavens
Parley's Natural Theology
Edwards On the Will
Allison of Taste
Moffat's Aesthetics
The Emotions by McCosh

Miss Bonney, pleasantly rotund and merry, held that marriage was the ideal vocation for young womanhood. Miss Dillaye was known for her dignity and cultured elegance. Once each year, Miss Dillaye would admonish the whole school: "Young ladies, aim at the moon and you will hit the church steeple, but if you aim at the church steeple you will hit the ground."

Commencement Day was also Examination Day for the Graduation Class. Parents and guests were assembled, and the Principals and the Examining Committee (composed of about eight distinguished clergymen) took their places. The graduates then came forward, one at a time, to draw from Miss Bonney a slip of paper. Each slip had written on it a subject of division of the text book, *Intellectual Philosophy*, on which the graduate was expected to recite. After all the girls had successfully completed the prerequisite, the diplomas were awarded. Later, at Ogontz, this examination was still conducted, but not before guests, making commencement a happier day for all.

By 1882 this school was one of the oldest girls' finishing schools in America and was attended by "young women" from all parts of the United States. By this time, it had outgrown its quarters and was looking for new ones. In the Fall of 1883 the school moved into "Ogontz," a mansion formerly owned by Jay Cooke, the prominent Civil War financier.

Centennial History of the University of Nebraska. I. Frontier University (1869-1969), by Robert N. Manley, University of Nebraska Press, 1969
Reproduced by permission of the University of Nebraska Press.

Chapter 11: The 1890's: A Time of Decision

[*Third paragraph*] Whether or not they were aware of the existing philosophical ferment [*about the role of land-grant universities and industrial training*], visitors to the campus in the 1890's were impressed by the earnest attitude of students and faculty. An air of purpose permeated the

buildings, and the ornate iron fence which surrounded the campus after 1891 seemed to proclaim that no outside distractions would be permitted to intrude upon those laboring within University Hall and the newer buildings were thronged with students pursuing a wide range of academic and practical courses. Professor H. H. Nicholson and a brilliant woman professor, Rachel Lloyd, who had joined the faculty in 1888 [*1887*], presided over the Chemical Laboratory. Newly built Grant Hall symbolized the land-grant university's devotion to the citizen soldier-scholar. And in Nebraska Hall, the home of the Industrial College, labored "the four busy B's — Bessey, Bruner, Brace and Barbour, whose names are household words in Nebraska." At night the campus was bathed in the glow of arc lights powered by the University's own generators and maintained by electrical engineering students.

Enrollment statistics show a gain during all but one year of this decade:

Academic Year	Number of Students
1890-1891	570
1891-1891	883
1892-1891	1,086
1893-1891	1,332
1894-1891	1,550
1895-1891	1,506
1896-1891	1,653
1897-1891	1,915
1898-1891	1,946

Chapter 13: Agricultural Education in the 1890s

[p. 140] As noted previously, Professor Thompson's early experiments with sugar beets were successful but met with no enthusiasm. However, by 1890 Nebraska had a thriving sugar-beet industry, due in large part to Professor Nicholson's work at the experiment station. He was joined in the work by Professor Rachel Lloyd, who was also on the agricultural staff at the Industrial College. No doubt farmers were leery of being instructed by a "female professor," but Professor Lloyd contributed significantly to Nebraska's sugar-beet industry. Impressed by the work of Nicholson and Lloyd, Chancellor Canfield asked Nebraska's Senator A. S. Paddock to apply to the United States Department of Agriculture for a fifty-thousand-dollar grant to establish a sugar school within the University. When no federal funds were made available, the University went ahead anyway. During the first session of the Sugar School, which was held in 1892 and lasted from January to May [*designed by Nicholson and Lloyd; taught to 35 students by Dr. Thomas Lyttleton Lyon, who was hired in 1891 after earning his Ph.D. at Cornell*], sugar-beet culture and manufacture were studied. The course was open to young men sixteen years of age and over. Graduates of the school were equipped to do the chemical work in sugar-beet factories, and were given the option of attending the farm in the summer to learn about the practical side of sugar-beet raising. The school was one of two in the nation, and as well as encouraging the development of Nebraska's sugar-beet industry, it pointed the way for the experimental work across the United States.

Women Scientists in America: Struggles and Strategies to 1940, by Margaret W. Rossiter, pp. 78-79. © 1982 Johns Hopkins University Press. Reprinted with permission of Johns Hopkins University Press.

Selection from
Chapter 4: A Manly Profession

Meanwhile the few women chemists in the country in the 1870s and 1880s (including once again Ellen Swallow Richards) were unable to get even this standard compromise of secondary membership in the new American Chemical Society, despite an encouraging beginning in 1874. In that year, when discussion in the *American Chemist* centered on how best to celebrate the upcoming centennial of the discovery of oxygen, Rachel Bodley, a graduate of the Wesleyan Female Seminary in Cincinnati and professor of chemistry and dean of the Women's Medical College of Philadelphia, wrote the journal to suggest that the chemists of America commemorate the occasion by meeting at Joseph Priestley's former home in Northumberland, Pennsylvania. Once assembled at that remote spot, the group voted to establish an American Chemical Society as soon as possible. The participants even showed their gratitude to Bodley for her suggestion by electing her one of the interim committee's thirteen honorary vice-presidents (the only woman so honored by the ACS before the 1970s). This recognition is all the more remarkable since Bodley did not bother to attend the meeting herself, preferring to spend the summer botanizing around Denver with friends. Several other women chemists did attend, however, including Ellen Swallow of MIT, Lydia Shattuck of Mount Holyoke Seminary, and Bessie Capen of the Girls' High School in Boston and later Wellesley College. But it was a danger signal in 1874 indicative of their marginal status in American chemistry that none of these three women was included in the famous photograph taken of the major participants at the Northumberland meeting (see plate 12). They were instead placed decorously off to the side, probably with the male scientists' wives and children.

Despite these three early participants and the honor afforded Bodley, no other women joined the ACS before the 1890s. One reason may have been the early society's preoccupation with industrial chemistry; another may have been its generally "clubby" atmosphere, which included stag dinners like that hosted by member Henry Morton, president of the Stevens Institute of Technology, at the annual meeting of the AAAS in Boston in August 1880. What makes this occasion different from many others like it was its ribald proceedings were taken down by a male stenographer, privately printed, and distributed to members as *The Misogynist Dinner of the American Chemical Society*. After this event, Bodley, the lone woman member, dropped out, and there were no women members until 1891, when Rachel Lloyd, assistant professor of analytical chemistry at the University of Nebraska, was elected. She was followed into the society shortly thereafter by Mary Engle Pennington, a recent doctorate from the University of Pennsylvania. By then, however, most women chemists were taking the men's hint and following Ellen Richards, who must surely have known of the misogynists' dinner in Boston in 1880, into the more womanly and receptive field of "home economics."

Journal of Chemical Education, vol. 59, p. 743
September 1982
[*The Tarbells wrote this article while preparing their 1986 book The History of Organic Chemistry in the United States, 1875-1955*]

Dr. Rachel Lloyd (1839-1900): American Chemist

by Ann T. Tarbell and D. Stanley Tarbell

Among the first women to publish in the *American Chemical Journal* was Rachel Lloyd, coauthor of three solid papers on acrylic acid derivatives with C. F. Mabery.

[*The full article is available online.*]

Sunday Journal and Star (Lincoln, Nebraska), p. 2D
October 24, 1982
Reproduced by permission of the Lincoln Journal Star.
[*This news article was prompted by the publication of the Tarbell's research on Rachel Lloyd in JCE*]

Rachel Lloyd Made Beets Crop Success

by Glenda Peterson

She was probably the first American woman to earn a doctorate in chemistry.

She was called "a brilliant professor" during her six years (1887-1894) on the University of Nebraska faculty.

And her painstaking, health-breaking sugar beet research at NU contributed significantly to what is now a multimillion-dollar industry in Nebraska.

Yet almost nobody has heard of Rachel Lloyd.

For 20 years, female staff members at the Nebraska State Historical Society have taken a special interest in women of Nebraska, but "the name (Rachel Lloyd) has never surfaced," says Betty Loudon, research associate for 16 years.

Lloyd's work is not indexed in the University of Nebraska-Lincoln chemistry department's card catalog of publications, nor can her name be found in a computer search of chemical literature. She is not listed in "American Men and Women of Science," "Chemists and Chemical Engineers," "Index of Scientists from Ancient to Modern Times," or "World Who's Who of Science."

Not in histories

Rachel Lloyd's name does not appear in the histories of Nebraska written by J. S. Morton, James Olson, Albert Watkins and Addison Sheldon; in "Nebraska Women Through the Years, 1867-1967," prepared under the direction of the Governor's Commission on the Status of Women; or in "Women of Nebraska Hall of Fame," for which 47 organizations submitted to the Nebraska International Women's Year Coalition the names of women who pioneered and helped develop the state and nation. (A retired chemistry professor said chemistry department scuttlebutt is that some male professors may later have taken credit for Lloyd's work.)

Her work is given credence and her departure from the university is lamented in Robert Manley's "Centennial History of the University of Nebraska, 1869-1969."

Yet 13 more years have passed since Manley's publication without further recognition being given to her teaching or research.

The significance of her scientific study now has surfaced, however, thanks to a husband-wife team at Vanderbilt University in Nashville, Tenn.

D. Stanley Tarbell, distinguished professor emeritus at Vanderbilt, in writing a history of organic chemistry in the United States, found that Lloyd was one of very few women to publish a chemical paper in the 1880s in a scientific journal, specifically the American Chemical Journal.

Wrote NU

He wrote NU seeking information on this rare 19th-century female chemist. Joe Svoboda, university archivist, wrote back: "Dr. Lloyd was professor of chemistry at the University of Nebraska from July 1887 to June 1894. Her annual salary was $1,500 a year. Her original title was associate professor of analytical chemistry — she was promoted to full professor in 1888. We also have in our files three publications authored by Lloyd relating to analyses of sugar beets."

Tarbell and his wife, Ann, writing in the September Journal of Chemical Education, note that Lloyd was born in 1839 in Flushing, Ohio. Her chemist husband, Franklin, died in 1865, after which she spent some time abroad, then taught at a private girls' school in Louisville, Ky.

Attended Harvard

She attended Harvard Summer School from 1876 to 1884 [*1875 to 1883*], then went to the University of Zurich, at that time the only place where women could work for a doctorate in chemistry. In Switzerland, she not only earned her doctorate (1886), but also became interested in sugar beets.

Accepting — by letter from London — NU's offer as associate professor of analytical chemistry, Lloyd came to NU about the time that the university was being transformed from "a small frontier college into a major institution," Manley wrote. There was "an earnest attitude" among students and faculty, and "an air of purpose permeated the buildings."

At the same time, Nebraska farmers were seeking diversification, trying, among other crop varieties, sugar beets and chicory.

Manley: Brilliant

Lloyd, whom Manley describes as "a brilliant woman professor," was appointed chemist to the Nebraska Agricultural Experiment Station, assisting H. H. Nicholson, who, with Lloyd, made up NU's two-member chemistry faculty.

Lloyd carried a heavy teaching schedule: five courses with lectures and 29 lab hours a week.

One of her students was Samuel Avery, whom she helped inspire to get a Ph.D. from Heidelberg. He later became professor of agricultural chemistry, chemist at the Nebraska Experimental Station and, eventually, chancellor of the university.

But it was in her sugar beet work at the experiment station that Lloyd made her greatest contribution to science and to Nebraska agriculture.

According to the Tarbells, the sugar beet industry was introduced to the United States after 1830, and two commercially successful beet sugar factories were established in California in 1879 and 1888.

"This promising cash crop and industry aroused the interest of the farmers around Grand Island, Nebraska," the Tarbells wrote. "However, wide variations in climate, soil, agricultural procedures and genetic characteristics of seed led to wide variations in the sugar content of the beets; therefore, it became one of the prime tasks of the experiment station to determine if Nebraska-grown beets were rich enough in sugar to warrant a sugar factory."

Trial Crops

Lloyd analyzed beets from the Grand Island trial crop in 1888 and reported a favorable outlook to the state Board of Agriculture.

She and Nicholson arranged for experimental plots at the new substations along railroad lines and enlisted the cooperation of many farmers.

After 700 analyses, with more than 2,000 farmers cooperating, Lloyd determined in 1889 that a sufficient percentage of the beets possessed the sugar content necessary for profit.

By 1890, according to Manley, Nebraska had a thriving sugar beet industry, largely because of Nicholson's and Lloyd's work.

"No doubt, farmers were leery of being instructed by a 'female professor,' but Professor Lloyd contributed significantly to Nebraska's sugar-beet industry," Manley wrote.

The favorable experiment station results influenced the Oxnard brothers, who were sugar technologists and refiners with experience in France and the United States, to build the nation's third successful beet sugar factory at Grand Island in 1890; a year later, a similar factory was built in Norfolk. "That's essentially how the sugar beet industry got started," Ann Tarbell said by telephone from Nashville.

Impressive fruition

The Tarbells say Nebraska's current sugar beet production is "impressive fruition of the labors of Nebraska's two chemists in the first years of the agricultural experiment station."

Because of declining health, Lloyd asked in 1894 to be given a lighter workload, but the university said it could not keep her under that arrangement. Another chemist with whom she worked, C. F. Mabery, wrote in 1901 that it was a pity that people were obliged to labor so hard that their health became impaired.

Lloyd died at Beverly, N. J., on May 7, 1900.

The Tarbells say Mabery wrote movingly of Lloyd's ability, remarkable energy, forceful character, attractive personality and sympathetic nature.

Acting Chancellor Charles E. Bessey, a former colleague at the experiment station, said of Lloyd in a memorial lecture: "She was not only an eminent chemist, she was a great teacher, and more than that, she was the beloved advisor and counselor of students."

The History of Organic Chemistry in the United States, 1875-1955, by Dean Stanley Tarbell and Ann Tracy Tarbell, Nashville: Folio Publishers, 1986

Chapter 6: Chemical Laboratories, Supplies, Instruction, Journals, Women Students to 1914

[*page 81*] Summer schools at the large universities provided oases for the teachers in small colleges. Reid, teaching at the College of Charleston and at Baylor, lamented his inability to plan research projects; his personal library was inadequate and little was available in the colleges. He welcomed summer school at Hopkins and Chicago for the purpose of library research. In small colleges it was not uncommon for the professor's own shelf to furnish the only reference books and journals. Rachael [*Rachel*] Lloyd performed her collegiate work in chemistry at the Harvard summer school, which began in 1874 and offered courses, laboratory instruction, and some summer teaching positions to chemists from smaller institutions. Louis J. Bircher, of Vanderbilt University, attended the summer sessions for many years at Chicago to achieve his Ph. D. in chemistry in 1924.

During this period another movement in education was reflected in the pages of the ACJ: the broadening of advanced education for women. Over thirty papers in organic chemistry were published with more than twenty women as co-authors between 1881 and 1913, and half as many again in other journals. In this progress Johns Hopkins was not a leader. Although by 1900 coeducation was widely accepted in the United States, Hopkins excluded women from its graduate school until 1907 and granted only two

Ph.D.s in organic chemistry to women, Bessie Brown and Julia Harrison, in this interval.

The first woman to publish organic chemistry in the ACJ was Rachel Lloyd, a co-worker with C. F. Mabery at Harvard Summer School for three years from 1881 [*actually seven out of eight years from 1872 to 1883*]. Lloyd took her Ph.D. at Zurich in 1886 [*1887*] and accepted an appointment at Nebraska to teach and to help establish the beet-sugar industry of that state; she rose to full professor in 1888. Scattered publications came from women in the Midwest and New England, where the women's colleges were training women in chemistry to teach chemistry or home economics in women's colleges or state institutions. A number of women took advanced degrees, taught, and performed research, for example, Dorothy Hahn (Ph.D. 1916, Yale) at Mount Holyoke in organic chemistry, and Jennie Tilt (M.S. 1910, Purdue) and Marie [*Mary*] L. Fossler (A.M. 1898, Nebraska) in physiological chemistry and nutrition. Helen Abbott Michael (the wife of Arthur Michael) was privately educated and widely traveled; between 1883 and 1896 she published fifteen papers on organic constituents of plants and in pure organic chemistry. Her account of visits to various European laboratories and their attitudes toward women students is enlightening. The most important centers in America for women in organic chemistry were Chicago, open to women since its inception in 1892, and Bryn Mawr College.

[*The book has much more about other chemists.*]

American Chemists and Chemical Engineers, Volume 2, Edited by Wyndham D. Miles and Robert F. Gould, Guilford CT: Gould Books, 1994, p. 167
[*Creese wrote this entry while preparing her four-volume series on women chemists of the world.*]

Rachel Abbie Holloway Lloyd
1839-1900
by Mary R. S. Creese

Rachel Lloyd, professor of analytical chemistry at University of Nebraska from 1887 to 1894, was probably the first American woman to be awarded a Ph.D. degree in chemistry.

[*The full entry is available in the book.*]

Bulletin of the History of Chemistry,
Volume 17/18, pages 9-14, 1995
*[Creese wrote this entry while preparing her four-volume series
on women chemists of the world.]*

Rachel Lloyd: Early Nebraska Chemist

by Mary R. S. Creese and Thomas M. Creese

In all likelihood Lloyd was the first American woman to take a Ph.D. in chemistry and the first to hold a full professorship in any science at a co-educational state university. She was in Nebraska for only seven years, her career being cut short by failing health, but the time was one of development and opportunity, and her contributions to the university and the regional agricultural community were notable. Her story has remained elusive, however; her early life unknown, and the question how she got her chance in Nebraska, a matter of special interest to students of the history of women in chemistry, has gone largely unasked.

[The full paper is available online.]

*Women in Chemistry: Their Changing Roles from Alchemical
Times to the Mid-Twentieth Century,* by Marlene and
Geoffrey Rayner-Canham, American Chemical
Society & Chemical Heritage Foundation, 1998,
pages 55-57

Rachel Lloyd (1839-1900)

Many pioneer women chemists embarked on a chemical career in life, only to move into other fields later. Lloyd, on the other hand, became a chemist only after the death of husband, Franklin, an industrial chemist.

[The full entry is available in their book.]

Adventures Abroad
by Sandra Singer, Praeger, 2003, p. 116

Women in Mathematics and Science
CHEMISTRY

She [*Rachel Lloyd*] became the second woman to earn a doctorate in chemistry in Europe and may have been the first American woman to earn a doctoral degree in chemistry anywhere.

[The book has short descriptions of many other women.]

About the Author

Mark Griep is a chemistry professor at the University of Nebraska-Lincoln. He studies the function of the enzymes that duplicate DNA in bacteria and is especially well known for his work with the enzyme named primase, the enzyme that starts the DNA duplication process. In the classroom, he has taught the entire range of courses from introductory chemistry for non-science majors to a graduate level course in chemical biology. He has also taught several honors courses including one for entering freshmen titled *The Color Red* that explored the abstract concept of "red" from nine academic perspectives. In 2007, he received an Alfred P. Sloan Award in the area of Public Understanding of Science to learn how chemistry and chemical imagery makes its way into the narrative of popular movies. In 2008, he received a Distinguished Teaching Award in recognition of his efforts to make chemistry understandable. In 2010, Oxford University Press published *ReAction! Chemistry in the Movies* that he co-authored with his wife Marjorie Mikasen. Since then, he has given several keynote lectures across the country about chemistry in the movies. In 2013, he began collaborating with Nebraska's two tribal colleges, Nebraska Indian Community College and Little Priest Tribal College, to connect their chemistry courses to local community topics. He has been studying his family history since age 13 and the history of his Department since 1997.

Made in the USA
Coppell, TX
11 March 2022